GOD

and

CHILDREN

GOD

and

CHILDREN

CʒᏸᎧ

Jesus Urteaga

Criterion
Lagos

Nihil Obstat: John V. Coffey, O. Carm., STL, censor theol. deput.
Imprimi Potest: ✠ Ioannes Carolus, Archiep. Dublinen
                   Hiberniae Primas
                   Dublini, Die 1 Iulii, anno 1965

Original title in Spanish:
Dios y los hijos (Ediciones Rialp, S.A., Madrid)

Translation by Leo Hickey

ISBN 978-36269-0-6

CRITERION PUBLISHERS LTD,
28, Ilorin Street, Surulere, Lagos.
email: info@criterionpublishers.org
website: www.criterionpublishers.org

Printed by:

TOMAKAN NIG. LTD.
16b, Oguntona Crescent, Gbagada Phase 1, Lagos.
Email: tomakanng@gmail.com

FOREWORD

The most notable tendency in theological writing in recent years has been one towards unity in theology itself. For too long a praiseworthy desire to order and detail the teaching of the Church had given rise to an increasing departmentalisation of theology, with the result that its different branches became more and more independent of each other. In particular, ascetical theology which deals with the practice of the faith and with growth in the interior life was separated from moral theology and from consideration of the place of the liturgy in the life of the individual Christian. Priest and layman both experienced difficulty in seeing the wood for the trees, and were hindered rather than helped in their understanding of the basic simplicity of the Gospel.

This fragmentary view has been considerably adjusted in the past twenty or thirty years by theologians and ascetical writers who have striven to emphasise the two most fundamental features of Christianity: the new Commandment – and it is still so new – of Love, and secondly, the universal calling to perfection. Without the desire of loving God and men, without having a Christ-centred religion in which everything is viewed in the light of personal friendship with our Lord, without perfecting and sanctifying oneself in one's ordinary life, religion can seem at least irrelevant and perhaps a nuisance: it is seen as nothing more than morality, and morality without love is indeed soul-destroying.

In his first book *Man, the Saint,* Father Urteaga wrote with great freshness and sincerity about the supernatural value of human virtues, about the ordinary life of a

Christian in the world. He wrote – and he still writes – enthusiastically and noisily. Does he generalise?

He would rather generalise than obscure his message by countless obvious qualifications. Does he become angry? Sometimes: but anger is a passion which, if controlled, can be very good, very manly and completely compatible with charity. These are matters of form, of style, which we can take or decline as we wish.

But his doctrine is not his own. In this book about the vocation of parents he outlines the Church's teaching on marriage and family life and shows how the love of Christ can, as it should, influence and transform both family and home into a way of sanctification and (the two things are the same) a way of happiness. Everything that he says is in the light of our Lord's invitation to all men to seek Christian perfection: 'You are to be perfect, as your heavenly Father is perfect' (Matthew 6, 48). He insists that love, human and supernatural, is opposed to a spirit of calculation, and in particular, at the beginning of his book, he shows how this love must, if it be true, respond generously to God's invitation to 'increase and multiply' (Genesis 1, 28).

What he has to say should be viewed in the light of a recent address by Pope Paul VI[1], in which the Pope goes beyond the moral implications of birth control and lays the stress not on avoiding what is illicit but on positively seeking what is good. The Pope greeted 'all those families whose fertility, crowned by a magnificent diadem of children, is an evident proof of their deep and serious concept of the family and of their living and conscious Faith'; and went on to say: 'Your presence in the world is a testimony of faith, courage and optimism; it is an act of vital and complete trust in the divine Providence and a clear exaltation of the highest and most noble values of the family and a proof of right moral conscience in a society and at a time that shows such alarming symptoms of selfishness, of indifference, of meanness.' Lastly, he pointed out the duty of Catholic parents to 'honour and respect the family in its primary end of being a blessed and fruitful source of human life.'

The Church's doctrine on birth control, then, must not be made a dessicated thing divorced from the love of God and the search for perfection. Catholics are not presented with a severe doctrine and nothing more. They are given high ideals and also the means to reach these through love and faith and hope. In the last analysis they are given these ideals by Christ and Christ is the most considerate, the most understanding, the most loving of Lords.

The greater part of the book is concerned with the education of parents and of children: very young children, the in-betweens and the adolescent; and in these chapters Father Urteaga draws heavily on his own rich experience as a teacher and spiritual director. To his subject he brings much doctrine, much humour and enormous common sense. These qualities combine to make *God and Children* a very valuable book for all parents and especially parents of young children.

FR RICHARD MULCAHY
Dublin, 23 April 1964

[1] Address to a Committee of the Association of Italian Families, 14 December 1963.

Contents

For Him who alone can work wonders with your children.

And for you, if your generous ambition is to help them become adults, Christians and saints. Is there any human task more noble or more beautiful?

If you help many children to reach heaven you will shine eternally, bright as the stars.

INTRODUCTION

GOD'S HOPE: YOUR CHILDREN

The first things that God looked at when he became a man on our earth were a mother's eyes.

Rejoice all of you who have children, for you have good cause to rejoice. Whoever you may be, you have responded to your vocation, you have answered the call from the Lord. You have cooperated with God in giving birth to your children. And he who began that good work will also complete it. Whether parents or friends, if you help many children to reach heaven, you will shine eternally, bright as the stars. 'Fatherhood itself is the Lord's gift . . . Children are like arrows in a warrior's hand. Happy, whose quiver is well filled with these; their cause will not be set aside' (cf Psalm 126).

I wrote to you some years ago: do you remember? It was a long letter in which I spoke to you about the divine value of human things.[1] I remember I did my best to reproduce for you as faithfully as possible the doctrine I had learned from the Founder of Opus Dei. And I spoke to you of those adventures that can be lived by every Christian in this world, which is so full of chaos: the adventure of work, the adventure of pain, the adventure of death. We spoke of many interesting and important things.

In that long letter, which I wrote to you from an old mill situated in Castille, in Spain,[2] I spoke of God and of men and of the many things we Christians have to achieve in this world of ours. I wrote with great enthusiasm and energy. I filled pages and pages, writing day and night. The whole thing took me only a fortnight to write, and all the time I was singing silently. The eyes of my imagination showed me many many men pass before me in a long parade, and I wrote only about what I saw. What I did, I think, was to show you what the men of this second half of the twentieth century should be like.

Anyone who opened that book by chance would say that we were crazy. And indeed the whole thing is a kind of craziness, a great craziness.

The world is steeped in darkness, and here we are speaking of a great Light which is pervading everything. Men speak of wars to come and of persecutions, while we talk about the great Peace which is approaching. Men shut themselves up in terror at the thought of the present, but we sing of joy and hope, looking to the future. Selfish people shut the gates of their soul and store up treasures on earth that rot away while we cry: 'It is worth while, it is worth giving up everything'!

How can we expect them not to say we are crazy when they just do not understand us, when they simply cannot understand us? – Although they certainly cannot say we do not proclaim our craziness aloud for all to hear. You and I will just go on, keeping our sights high.

You notice there are people watching us jealously and with very much suspicion from near and far. Never mind; there have always been people like that, they were there even at the very beginning of Christianity. They are not Christians, so how can we expect them to be pleased at our triumphs and progress? The Lord has taught us to do what we are doing. So, forward without fear!

Gossip and what people may say are of no importance. John came, neither eating nor drinking, and they said he was possessed by the devil. Jesus came; he ate bread and drank wine, and because of that they called him a glutton and a drunkard. They are as illogical and inconsistent as children; when we pipe songs of joy to them, all they do is cry (this is Christ's comment, not mine).

Just wait and have confidence. Even the indifferent will come over to our side. You do not realise the full value of Love. They will come to the Light out of curiosity, if nothing else, and then the Truth, with its impetus, will sweep them forward with the rest of us.

Well, now that I have mentioned something of this great adventure which is spreading rapidly throughout the world, this idea of perfection for everyone, I want to get down to the subject of this book. Forgive me for spending so long over the preliminaries. It is a long time since I wrote you that first letter; in fact some years have passed since then, and now I find you settled down to a new way of life: with a home, a wife and children. Perhaps I should say too that you seem a bit older. But to get down to the subject. I want to speak to you now of a great task, a great undertaking.

Do you know why great tasks and great undertakings fail?

There are so many people nowadays, good people, who want to do great things for Christ. They start off with enthusiasm, great resolutions and sufficient means; soon after beginning, many companions have joined them. But then, unfortunately, they think they can do everything at once. So their downfall is tremendous and complete.

According as these new movements appear, the older ones die out. And when the new ones disappear, still others come to take their place. Do you see now why there is so much failure in the great enterprises that men undertake? It is simply this: they lack supernatural and human judgment, principles, standards. They all try to begin at the top, forgetting the most elementary rule of architecture which is that they must begin at the bottom. What can we do with strong well-made roofs if there are no walls and no pillars to support them?

You and I are going to begin now at the bottom, on a good solid foundation. This foundation is Christ himself, and there can be no other foundation for a Christian life. The undertaking I want to speak to you about in this book is an enormous one. So we have to begin at the bottom: with Christ and with your home.

I am much more concerned about the home, your home, than about whatever bad or dangerous atmosphere you may find in the street. I am much more worried about the way of life your children will learn in your home, following your example all the time, seeing you live your life, than I am about anything they may learn from the faithlessness and faults of others. What I am not so sure about is whether you are capable of giving them that 'something' – and it is a very great something – which they have to get if they are to live Christian lives.

Just think of the type of world we can and will create for the people of tomorrow if only we get these children of yours to understand, to realise fully, from this moment on, that Christ is really alive; that they must serve the Church and be ready to lose everything, their wealth, their honour and their life, if necessary; that Christ has certain rights in our human society, rights which only the ignorant or the dishonest can deny him, rights which must be protected and enforced, and that Christians must take an active part in public life, so as not to let that true Life be suffocated and buried, hidden away in men's consciences.

Do you realise the great things we will achieve tomorrow – and I mean a tomorrow which is already dawning – if we make the effort now to train and educate our children, our men, as God and his Church want us to train and educate them? They must be faithful men, determined, strong-willed, enterprising, responsible, hard-working, freedom-loving, fearless, without any inhibitions, without any silly scruples, afraid of nothing; men of faith, of hope, of love, with a great love, a vigorous charity that will spur them into action, from feeding the hungry to waking up all those around us who are asleep and in danger of losing their place in heaven, for indeed there are many of these.

It is from these children, your children, that God hopes for great things. Now are you beginning to see what I want to speak to you about in this book?

But why do you lapse into such morose silence? Does the task before you seem light, or does it seem too heavy and therefore impossible? Remember we have God on our side. And 'who is like the Lord our God? . . . He gives the barren woman a home to dwell in, a mother rejoicing in her children' (Psalm 112). You have every reason to be optimistic.

TO PARENTS

It is for you, who are the father or mother of a family, that I am writing all this. I have many things to say to you, to all of you who feel – as you must feel – joy, delight and happiness in being able to cooperate with God in the birth and upbringing of your children; to all of you who cherish the generous ambition of bringing up men who will be faithful, fully developed, trustworthy, ready to commit themselves in the eyes of God and of the world.

I want to speak, too, to those of you who know from experience the sorrows that life can bring, and who want your children to turn away from the call of sin.

I am writing also for those of you who want to begin anew, because you are weighed down heavily with the burdens of life. To you I can show a new way of life, so that your children will have nothing to be sorry for at the end of their time on earth.

And I am writing also for you, my good friend, and for all like you who have suffered, alone and in silence, when their longed-for child was born . . . but born blind. Yes, I do fully understand the sorrow you pour out to me in your letter. Please regard this book as my reply. I fully understand how sad you are . . . but I do not pity you, I will not pity you. The Lord has treated you as one of his strong and healthy children because he is not afraid of seeing you weep, although, as you admit in your letter, 'sometimes the cross becomes very heavy.' Let me tell you with Saint Teresa: 'Those whom God loves well, he leads by ways strewn with toil, and the more he loves them the greater the toil.'

As a Christian and as a friend I can promise you that your Father God relied and is relying on that blind son of yours to do great things, perhaps to bring the Light to the eyes of many men on earth. Do not think me heartless: indeed I have a very soft heart, and I am weeping with you in your misfortune, believe me. But I must tell you, as a Christian, as a friend and as a priest, that your child's blindness is something good. I will help you to use all the means possible, human and supernatural, to cure him. And I will celebrate it with you if some day he recovers his sight. But if God, our good Father God, decides that his eyes are to be opened only when he reaches heaven, then I will help you to give thanks because 'for those who love God everything is for the good' (Rom 8,28).

And to you too, you wretched coward, I want to speak, to you who are so delighted by and enjoy yourself so much with your children that you are terrified by the thought that some day something is bound to go wrong.

You give the impression of being afraid to speak aloud of the joy you derive from your family, as if you had escaped all the sorrow which the Lord has to bestow. Do you think for one moment that God does not know what is in store for you? Lift up your head and thank him for the gift he has given you. Any other attitude is merely ridiculous and even superstitious. Be happy with your children and dream about them as much as you like, but never forget to give thanks to your God. Why then that furtive look? Do you think he does not want us to be happy in this world?

And to you also, who are now without children because the Lord took them from you before you could feel the joy of having them. I am writing for you, knowing that God will give you another joy.

I am writing for all those who have or would like to have children. In this book I can say nothing to those who have none because our Father God – and I hope you realise by now how good this Father of ours is – does not want you to have them. But those who have no children because, through their own wickedness, they have brutally blocked the sources of life had better not bother to read what I have to say; for I am going to speak about Love, and those people do not understand what that word means. They think it means flesh, and it is true that it has that meaning . . . but only in hell. What they should do is repent, try to undo the damage they have done and change their way of life.

I was really upset when that old man finished speaking, with the words: 'My hands are empty and I am afraid, very much afraid, of death.' Without any idea that I was saying the wrong thing, I answered him sincerely, straight from the heart: 'But you have ten children. They are ten good deeds which will count in your favour to get into heaven.' With infinite sadness he answered me: 'No, that is not so. I had those children in the days when we had none of those methods we have now. Otherwise I wouldn't have had them at all.'

There followed an embarrassing silence, which I can still feel. I remember well the tree that old man was leaning against; and I remember how the other trees around were looking at us. And the old man, the tree and I were all filled with a kind of bitter sadness.

But forget all that now. I want you to be happy as you read this book. And you have reasons, good reasons, to be happy. Forget, if only for an hour or two, all those worries that pour into your soul every day. Take that tired look off your face. I want you to be happy. Yes, indeed, you have every reason to be happy.

God has entrusted some men with the destiny of nations; to others he has committed the task of achieving great things, divine or human; he leads some along wide and pleasant paths, while others he takes through monotonous ways and arduous roads in this world with a promise of great things in the next; others . . .

You too he may have chosen for these or other similar tasks, I do not know; but besides that, and much more important, he has placed in your hands – you yourself know whether they are clean hands – the lives of a few children, little angels or little rascals as the case may be, and you will have to give a serious and sincere account of that task when he calls you to judgment, at the end of these few years which slide by as we grow old and pass through the world. 'Only then will we see clearly', said Father Garrigou-Lagrange, 'all that was demanded of us by our particular and individual vocation: as a mother, as a father, as an apostle.'

Be happy, father, mother, apostle, for God asked you to collaborate with him. Many great things can be done in this life; but there is none so great, so noble, so beautiful as this: to help your child to become a man, a Christian, a saint.

Yours is a great and sublime mission, you who are a mother, because the glory of your children will be your glory too. Many things were left unsaid by that woman in the Gospel who was so impressed with Christ and so full of praise for his mother: 'Blessed is the womb that bore thee.' Blessed indeed are those mothers who try to bring up their children in a Christian manner.

Yours is a mission of sacrifice, you who are a father, because there will be many days on which the fruit of your work will not be seen at all. Your attitude and mine must be completely self-sacrificing, completely disinterested, for we have to stand aside and let them go their own way in life, after giving them our lives little by little, day after day. It is a mission that is very great, very noble, very beautiful . . . and very worrying. The responsibility that you carry on your shoulders is tremendous, and it is a responsibility which you can neither escape nor lighten.

Tell me, has the education of your children any other purpose than to help them to become other Christs? Answer that question, and then remind yourself that Christ died, hanging from a cross, on Good Friday evening.

Yes, you will have to go through trials, sorrows and fears; through discouragement, uneasiness, cares and worries; but you will also have great ambition and great hopes. You will experience great joys and great delights; you will fulfil great dreams and see achievements. Undoubtedly you will yield fruit.

It is ten years since I last wrote to you. I wrote to you then, as I said, in an old mill, bathed in the scorching sun of Castille. But I am writing this in different surroundings: in a big Basque house, called Gaztelueta,[3] enveloped in mists coming in from the sea. I have more than 270 youngsters all around me. If there are splashes of ink on this paper it is not my fault; and if you find that from time to time I lose my train of thought, you must blame no one but those children who are here with me, taking away all my trains of thought, all my sweets, all my patience and all my good intentions of revising what I write.

You must not think that this book will give you concrete solutions to little pedagogical problems. You can get those somewhere else; there are many very good books written to help you solve those problems.

I am going to talk to you only about God and about your children.

I think you will find, if you look back, that you have been guided through the whole of your life by a few rules your own parents taught you. Well, those are the things I want to talk to you about, those few things that are so forgotten nowadays.

I want to speak to you about the great principles which should direct your own life, the life of your home and the life of your children, so that you and they may be called, in the fullest meaning of the phrase, children of God.

[1] *Man, the Saint,* 3rd ed., Scepter, Chicago and Dublin, 1963.
[2] A reference to 'Molinoviejo', a conference centre run by Opus Dei near Segovia.
[3] A day-school run by Opus Dei near Bilbao.

LIVING HOMES AND DEAD HOMES

LIVING HOMES

There should be nothing dead about your home. How often we find dried-up sponges in Holy Water fonts!

Later on I will speak to you about your duty to have children; but first of all I want to speak to you about the home, and more particularly about living homes. You will see what I mean. We need homes with an atmosphere that is healthy, strong, affectionate and manly, human and supernatural, in which the children will be brought up, not just to resist the evil influence of the pagan world, but so that they themselves will transform that world in accordance with the divine plan.

My heart always goes out to those first Christian homes which were born and nurtured in the warmth of Jesus' own words, in which the faith of the new converts was fully lived. They still kept alive in the atmosphere of those homes the life-giving echo of the Lord's words when he said: 'Love one another, love one another.' And lest anyone should forget what Jesus commanded, John repeated it again from the island of Patmos: 'Love one another, that you may love one another.' And all the apostles taught the same message: 'Love one another, love one another.'

Is there anything more alive, more living, than love? And how those first few loved one another!

You cannot hope to make a home like they did, merely by hanging things on the wall. No, homes are not brought to life simply by adding more things; it is not a question of adding anything, like pictures on a wall. Christian families, like the mustard seed, grow from inside outwards. You will never get roses to bloom by pulling their petals.

In the atmosphere of a Christian family time alone, even without any conscious effort on anyone's part, will make the whole of that Life, which the people who dwell there carry within them, burst out into the open, flourish and blossom into full bloom. But if there is no Christian fibre in the man and woman of the house, then it will produce nothing but leaves. For Christianity, of its very essence, is a living organism.

Now look: we are not trying to produce good or even very good homes, with a certain standard of external decency, decorum or honour. Believe me, what we are trying to achieve is much more than that. Remember it is from our homes that we hope – and have every reason to hope – to restore Christianity to the world. So what we want to implant in the world has first to be grafted into these homes of ours. It is in the large Christian families that we will find the support needed for the great evolution the world of today has to undergo.

With those Christian families we shall form men who will go out and work to achieve the triumph of Christ in every aspect of human activity. And even a single home can do so much! But you do not fully realise that, do you?

Give me Christian homes, and I shall no longer be frightened by the pagan streets. Give me Christian homes, and I shall not worry about the evil atmosphere which surrounds us on all sides. Give me Christian homes, and I shall cease to fear the current entertainments or the beaches. Give me Christian homes, and the Godless schools will no longer terrify me.

But if we have no homes in which the parents genuinely form Christ in their children, then I fear, I greatly fear, the streets, the beaches, the atmosphere, the entertainments and the Godless schools.

At times I wonder if you have any understanding at all of what God wants you to do with your home. I see that you are anxious to make men of your children, and that is good. But, really, is it enough?

'Christianity proclaims in a supremely emphatic manner something new, a new relationship concerning what is most intimate in human nature, and this is valid both in time and in eternity. To "be a Christian" is something new, something completely different, something vastly superior to merely "being a man". In becoming a Christian a new vital order begins in the fullest sense of the word' (Schumacher).

We need Christian homes, living, vigorous, energetic, Christian homes, like the home of Lazarus, Martha and Mary, like the home of the parents of James and John, like the home of Peter and Andrew, like the home set up by the centurion at Capharnaum together with his servants. The more Christian your home is, the more similar will it be to the home at Nazareth.

I insist again on this idea of 'Life', because that is the summing up and the synthesis of the whole of Christianity. 'I have come', Christ tells us, 'that they may have life, and have it more abundantly.'

So how can we be content now with what we see in our homes? How can you, parents, react like that? Is that the life that Christ brought with him? Certainly it is not; we cannot but rebel against this inert and useless attitude. Christ could never have come down on earth to teach us what we see practised in these homes of ours.

Our children receive Communion daily, because it is interesting and easy, but when they reach the age of eighteen or so they begin to receive only five times a year. They go to Confession on Saturday, receive Communion on Sunday morning and crucify Christ that same evening. But this is simply monstrous. No, that was certainly not the life that Christ brought us.

You must never forget, or let your children forget, that our Father God sent Christ to our homes so that we should live by him. All Christians are children of God, and this is no mere metaphor or manner of speaking, but a vital fact. We are born of God, and the world is ours to conquer. We are born of God, however poetical or oratorical this may sound.

'We are from God, we are from God', is the cry we hear from John the evangelist. We are from God even if we behave like Nicodemus who had no idea how he could be born again into life.

We need living homes, where the children will realise that they have been delivered from death, real death, to life. You know that when we receive the water of that first Sacrament, we receive also the Holy Spirit. So why do you forget that all Christians have been born again, have risen from death to life?

We must offer ourselves and our homes to the Almighty, as people who were dead and have returned to life.

It was the blood of our Christ that sanctified us.

If you live and put into practice in your homes the doctrine taught by Christ, you will find that you have scarcely to say anything to make that home really come to life. Live that doctrine, parents; live as people who have returned to life. Live in Christ, who remains alive in your home.

Sow these ideas in the minds of your children, and you will reap eternal life for yourselves and for them. Make an effort to have the life of Christ lived in your home, and neither the rain, nor the wind, nor the floods will have any effect on it, because it will be built on solid rock.

CHRIST IN YOUR HOME

You must treat Christ as a very important person who sits down to table with you, as he sat with his disciples on the way to Emmaus, with Simon the pharisee, with Lazarus and his sisters.

You must regard him as a very important person who sleeps among you, as he slept in Peter's boat on that day when the storm arose over the lake.

You must treat him as someone who is in love with your children, remembering how affectionate he was towards those children whom he blessed when they went near him.

Do not fall into the temptation of thinking that God is too great to worry about the little material problems of your children.

You must treat him like a very important person who knows the pains of a mother giving birth to her child; as a person who understands the worry of a woman who has lost some money; as a person who feels compassion for a mother on the death of her son. For Christ was never unmoved by any sorrow, any pain, any sadness.

You must treat him as someone who can cure the leprosy, blindness, deafness or death of the soul.

That is how you must treat him; and if you do that, your children will learn to live with him as with a good friend, with a brother whom they love with a genuine love, with an affectionate father who is deeply interested in them, with a God who became a man because his delight was to be with the children of men.

Then, once you live in that way, all those pictures and statues you have hanging on the walls will take on a new meaning and will help your children to be more conscious of the presence of the living God. Then, a glance at the figure of Christ looking down on us from the Cross will be sufficient to remind us that 'love is deeds, not sweet words.'

A home is alive when the spirit of faith, the spirit of hope and the spirit of love is lived in it. Do you know how you can be sure that the home is alive as Christ wishes it to be? Well, 'by their fruits you shall know them.'

If you regard the birth of a new child as a blessing from God, then Christ is there beside the new creature. If your reaction to the death of a child is a Christian reaction, then Christ is there beside the little body. If you keep your temper and peace of mind in times of difficulty, then Christ is there behind your sorrow. In those cases I shall believe that your home is a living one.

Look at the life that flourished in those first homes set up under the hand of Christ. Aristides tells us: 'When a child has been born to one of them [the Christians], they give thanks to God; and if moreover it happens to die in childhood, they give thanks to God the more, for one who has passed through the world without sins . . . Such is, O King, the commandment of the law of the Christians, and such is their manner of life.'

You who are Christian parents, and we priests of the living God, how grave will be our responsibility if, for lack of effort on our part, we allow these children to have only a vague or not very clear notion of God!

How grave our responsibility if we abandon them to the erroneous influence of those who think that God is far away, too far to be concerned about us down here.

How grave our responsibility, yours and mine, if we allow them to imagine that he is indifferent to any of their problems.

How grave our responsibility if they do not learn to treat Christ, with the affection of children, as a very important person in heaven and on the earth.

The Lord speaks thus to us through the mouth of Isaias: 'Can a woman forget her infant, so as not to have pity on the son of her womb? And if she should forget, yet will not I forget thee. Behold, I have graven thee with my hands.'

You have to teach them the following – and remember it is not a parable, but an historical event. Jesus was invited to have a meal at the house of Simon the pharisee and he could not understand the inconsiderate and impolite way he was treated by the rich man. The good manners which it was customary to show to important guests at that time were not shown to him, the Lord. His feet were not washed; he was not given the formal kiss of greeting, nor was his head anointed with oil. The reason for this bad manners neither you nor I can understand; nor did Christ understand it; but, however, he let it pass. He asked nothing out of the ordinary, but merely what was customary in the place at that time. Do not forget that Christ was the Master, the Prophet, a very important person who condescended to eat in the house of Simon the pharisee.

Jesus wants to be treated at least as we would treat one of the important persons of this world: surely that is not asking too much?

Therefore when a woman approached the table, a woman who had been living a bad life but was now inwardly repentant, Christ let her perform those acts of politeness which were neglected by the rich host.

In front of the stupefied eyes of those who knew her, sobbing aloud, the poor woman poured over the Lord's feet an alabaster box of ointment, a perfume made of balm mixed with tears. She was not very sure of what she was doing; she wept, kissed his feet, dried them with her hair, kissed them again, poured out the perfume. Those tears would have moved any normal person, but they only hardened Simon's heart all the more.

And he was so hardened that he began to think: Is this Jesus, the Prophet? Does he not know what type of woman it is who is touching him?

And our Christ, who was willing to overlook the bad manners at the beginning of the meal, would not tolerate that vile impertinence.

'Dost thou see this woman?' he said to Simon. 'I came into thy house, and thou gavest me no water for my feet; she has washed my feet with her tears, and wiped them with her hair. Thou gavest me no kiss of greeting; she has never ceased to kiss my feet since I entered; thou didst not pour oil on my head; she has anointed my feet, and with ointment. And so, I tell thee, if great sins have been forgiven her, she has also greatly loved' (cf Luke 7, 40-47).

Parents and children, will you now learn how to treat Christ? You who receive him in the Holy Eucharist into the little home of your heart, do you receive him at least as you would receive a very important person who decided to visit you?

DIVINE FILIATION

'It is the mind of the Church that a truly Christian home is the atmosphere in which the children's faith is nurtured, grows and develops, and in which they learn, not only to be men, but to be children of God' (John XXIII).

Some pages back I told you that we had to construct a great edifice, and at the beginning of this book I mentioned the wonderful enterprise you have to undertake with your children. Now let us speak of the very foundation of the Christian life, yours and your children's.

First of all, let me ask you what, in your opinion, is the one great truth on which you should base all the convictions of your interior life. What is to be the centre around which the Christian life of your children has to revolve? What is the central idea which you, and they, have to foster above all others so that your life and theirs may grow, develop, flourish and yield the fruits which God expects from you?

There are many people who think themselves wise and knowledgeable but who would be unable to answer that question. This is so because, through speaking all the time about matters that are of little or no importance, they forget the really transcendental things.

Now there is only one true basis for the whole of our Christian life.

Your children have been brought forth into supernatural life by God. And they must live, therefore, as such children of God. This is the basis which is to support the whole weight of a genuinely Christian life: divine filiation.

This divine filiation must not be understood as something that is only morally true: it is not that we call ourselves children of God because he treats us like a good father. No, divine filiation involves something which makes us like unto him in such a real way that we 'are to share the divine nature' (2 Peter 1, 4). This is the mysterious gift, the unfathomable gift, that the Lord has bestowed on us!

A SIMPLE INTERIOR LIFE

Parents, you must simplify your own and your children's interior life. You must be careful not to tie them up in a kind of routine and cold piety of devotions and prayers, which mean nothing to children. Do not burden their lives with many isolated acts of piety, for this will only make them lose sight of the overall picture of sanctity. These are the ideas, perhaps, which will be kept and put into practice by your children all through their lives.

They are children of God, so they should go to him continually. This is the beginning of their life of prayer they should speak to God about all their affairs, with simplicity and sincerity, just as they speak to you. They should speak to him in that way when they get up in the morning, at meal times, when they go to bed at night, when they are going out of the house, when they begin to play and when the time comes to put the toys away. They must keep their Father God present with them at all times.

They are children of God, so you must teach them those vocal prayers which will be so important during their childhood and also afterwards in the formation of their interior life.

They are children of God, so they should have a great love for his mother, who is their mother also.

They are children of God, so they should live an intensely sacramental life.

Your children will have understood the meaning of divine filiation when they live a life of abandonment in the arms of their Father, that abandonment which is the secret of happiness (cf *The Way*, 853). This abandonment has nothing to do with passivity, with remaining inactive; it requires an effort on our part, because it implies developing our faith to the fullest – in other words, growing in our interior life – and also it means developing our natural gifts, with the help of grace; it involves developing all those human virtues I spoke to you about in my first book; and from this abandonment there will spring an unshakeably serene and calm disposition which will make your children always act calmly and without losing their supernatural outlook; it is an abandonment which always brings peace; it is an abandonment which gives, as its fruit, mastery over oneself and dominion over all external things.

If your children learn to live this divine filiation – first, of course, you must live it – they will never experience either discouragement, or sadness, or fear, or terror. They will realise that they are children of God. And for him, the Almighty, there are no obstacles, no difficulties. We can do all things, we repeat with Saint Paul, in him who gives us strength.

All those weaknesses common in the children of men will be made up for by the Holy Spirit, if only we are faithful to him.

If you and your children go deeply, or even try to go deeply, into the significance of the fact that you are children of God, then you will realise that you and they can give a divine value to every act you perform during the day, even the most ordinary, the most tiny, the most trivial.

And the deep significance of our whole asceticism is rooted in this fact. Everything you do, everything your youngest child does, can all be made divine, can be given a divine value. There is nothing valueless, absolutely nothing contemptible, in anything we do, if we remain, as good children of God, in his grace.

We must keep this fact always in mind; it will be an immense help to us. What we give the Lord will not be limited to a few, or even to many, periods of prayer. Everyday life becomes divine when the person living that life is a son of God. Everything changes into prayer, into love, peace, joy. Help your children to seek and find God in every circumstance.

DEVOTIONS: FEW, STRONG, CONSTANT

This is what your children should do.

When they get up in the morning, being children of God, they should say 'good morning' to him, but first jumping out of bed at the exact time. Make sure the devil of laziness does not overcome them: remember God is waiting. This 'good day' does not necessarily have to take any special form. It consists of offering him everything they are going to do during the day, whether it appears bright or gloomy. A 'good day' offered up to God or to his Mother; Jesus is glad when we sing to Mary. Get them used to praying in the morning, at the start of each new day. Many people have been taught to pray only when they are going to bed; but surely it is not very good manners for a child to say no more than 'good night' in the whole of the day.

Having a fixed vocal prayer for the morning offering has the advantages – provided of course that it is not said just out of habit – of being a great aid to the children's piety and giving them something they can remember with pleasure throughout their life.

It is a Christian custom, not only to ask the Lord to bless the food that we are going to accept as a gift from him, but also to thank him for all the good things he has granted us. The first Christians did this. 'Every morning and every hour they give thanks and praise to God for his loving-kindness towards them; and for their food and their drink they offer thanksgiving to him' (Aristides).

Whatever else you do, be sure to teach your children to be grateful, because Christ wants us to thank him for the favours we receive. Do you remember the episode of the ten lepers? The Lord was going into a town. He saw standing far away from him the carcasses, the rotting bodies, of ten lepers. They bared their heads, tore off their clothes and begged him to have mercy on them. He was moved to pity and sent them off to show themselves to the priests, and on the way they were cured by his power. Only one of those lepers came back to thank him. 'Where are the other nine?' he asked.

Nine out of ten of the lepers of all ages still show no gratitude to the Lord.

This is another good reason why you should teach your children – by your example – to give thanks to Jesus after receiving Holy Communion. What a great opportunity you have when you accompany them to the altar to receive that Sacrament.

One day you can get them to recite slowly those prayers blessed by the Church, which are to be found in every missal. Other days you can compose a new prayer in your own words, words worthy of a Christian father or a Christian mother. This morning, remembering that the Blessed Trinity, Father, Son and Holy Spirit have taken up their abode in your soul and in the soul of that child whom you love, you tell God that you never want to leave him by committing mortal sin. And your child repeats that prayer after you, pronouncing the words as best he can. And those words ring as melodious bells in heaven. Your child notices that today you have not repeated the same prayers as usual. Today you have really spoken to someone, to someone very important. In this way your children will begin to understand that no formulas or set words are necessary to tell Jesus how much they love him.

Take advantage of those moments during the thanksgiving after Communion to teach them to call the Lord by his name, Jesus (cf *The Way*, 303), to draw near to God with great confidence, to tell him about their needs, to ask forgiveness for the many defects and stains they have on their soul.

Another day You can let the child himself talk, in silence, to the Lord. These are the first meetings of your child with the Child Jesus.

If your children learn to pray with simplicity now, they will continue to treat the Lord with sincerity and naturalness all through their life, with no affectation, no mere formulas, no mere repetition of habits. If you know how to treat him properly, they too will learn how to treat him properly. They will be influenced by your life and infected with the wonderful infection of your love. Like that other child in his act of thanksgiving after Communion, who was asked by his father:

'What do you say to Jesus?'

'I love you', replied the child.

'And what else?'

'I look at him.'

The father was very moved by this living faith in his son, kissed him on the forehead, and asked:

'Do you think God is pleased by that?'

And again the child's faith burst out, for he had learned well the lesson of divine filiation:

'Aren't you pleased when I tell you I love you and when I look at you?'

Parents, begin to speak to them about Jesus as soon as you feel they can understand what you say.

Mother, take your beloved child by the hand and teach him to make the sign of the Cross on his little body, but make sure he does it properly. Speak to him of Jesus. Tell him the wonderful story of that God become a man.

Teach him to pray vocally and mentally. Show him how Jesus wants us to ask God for the things we need in this world: with humility and constancy, with perseverance, like the man who went in the middle of the night and woke up a friend of his to ask him for some bread. 'I tell you', Jesus teaches us, 'even if he will not bestir himself to grant it out of friendship, shameless asking will make him rise and give his friend all that he needs.'

One little boy had understood perfectly the significance of being in front of the Tabernacle. He met a friend of his in the chapel while they were both saying their penance after Confession. One was seven, the other eight. Suddenly the lights went out and the chapel was in darkness, but not complete darkness because there was a little light, the sanctuary lamp as always, showing that the Lord was there, a little flickering light throwing gigantic shadows on the reredos behind the altar. The older of the two, with a fantastic imagination, was afraid of the dark, and ran out into the passage. In a breathless voice he said:

'I'm scared.'

Then the little fellow came up behind him and calmly, quietly, with words full of faith, told him:

'You're silly. How can you be afraid in the chapel when Jesus is there?'

You're silly: I must say the same thing to you whenever I see you, father or mother, hesitate or be afraid in the face of human difficulties, little moments of darkness in your life; you are silly, very silly. You are with God: how can you be afraid?

Those who have little love of God pray to him in the morning and then forget about him until night.

This fact, that we are children of our Father God, will become the life of your children's life; they will begin to feel that they want to raise their heart to God at every moment of the day, by means of little aspirations, acts of love, little sacrifices, by constantly keeping in mind the presence of God, at their work, at their play, at the moment of obedience, at the time of the bath or when asking you to forgive them for the bad thing they did last night.

Teach them how we must keep the presence of God in mind in our everyday work, without any need to close our eyes or put ourselves in any special position. Tell them, on the contrary, to keep their eyes wide open, as Mary did at the feast in Cana. At that wedding feast, as always, the Blessed Virgin was living a contemplative life, a contemplative life which makes her miss no detail of everything going on at the table. It was she, the good Mother, who noticed that the wine was running short, and it was she who saved the situation by putting the matter entirely in the hands of her Son.

Any attempt to keep a presence of God which distracts you from your study or work, is a misguided attempt. Blessed are the eyes that see . . . And you and your children will see God in your life and in everything around you.

Let your children make resolutions for today – never make them think of tomorrow, because children have little regard for such abstract concepts – but do not force them to tell you what these resolutions are, if you see that they want to keep them secret.

Encourage them to lead a life of sacrifice, but not to keep a strict account of all the little sacrifices they make.

Help them to put their mortifications in order. In the first place, far above and more important than any personal penances, they must put those which help the welfare of others. If the child decided to eat something she does not like, very good, it will strengthen her will: but to give up her doll to let others play with it is a much better mortification. To say seven hundred Hail Marys in a week is a very good thing, but get them to have it very clear in their minds that if a situation arises in which they must choose between obeying you and saying the Hail Marys, then it is much better to obey.

Get your children to have a simple interior life, I must stress this again. Do not give them too many mortifications. By your own example, encourage their generosity and let the grace of God act in them from then on.

There was one very enthusiastic but not very prudent mother who thought she was doing the right thing – and this is so often the danger! – in giving her son Johnny a big box of chocolates on the morning of his First Communion. But the gift, as we shall see, was only a trick to encourage him to practise the spirit of sacrifice and generosity.

'This little box of chocolates' – in fact it was enormous – 'is a present for you', she said.

That was a good beginning to the celebrations for Johnny, as his eyes opened wide at the sight of the box. But then the mother began her lesson on generosity.

'Come on, Johnny; bring the box over here and give this lady a chocolate. You cannot eat them all yourself.' The child was not very pleased with that idea; he had quite definitely intended to eat them all himself. As he opened the box, he was saying to himself:

'Why did she give them to me then? Of course I must give three or four to Jimmy, he gave me his pictures the other day. Three for Charlie, no, two will do him; I don't like him at all. Mary will take at least five, whether I give them to her or not. She's all right, I like her. Yes, I'll give her five. And if I don't give them to her she'll take them anyway . . .'

This was Johnny's generous or not so generous way of thinking.

But the mother's way of thinking was rather different:

'Come on, Johnny. Let's go to visit your cousins.'

'All of them?'

Clutching the box with one hand, he counts on the fingers of the other:

'Seven, eight, nine . . . three each . . . Twenty seven! That's the end of my chocolates.'

And he puts one in his mouth, thinking it may be his last.

Again the voice calls him:

'Johnny!'

'Mummy again, shouting at me to be generous, I suppose', growls the child. And he is right; the mother comes into the room with a neighbour, whom he has to kiss. He says nothing, but his face shows what he is thinking: 'You have my chocolates all over your cheek; you didn't even give me time to wipe my mouth with my handkerchief. But that's not going to satisfy you: you'll want two more of my sweets. Poor box, and it was so big!'

A few minutes later when the mother appears with a child he has never before seen in the house, all the anger and annoyance built up in him by these robberies of which he has been the victim burst out in the eyes of poor Johnny, and before his mother can 'invite' him to be generous again, he throws the box into the hands of the newcomer and shouts:

'If you gave me the chocolates just to hand them out to everyone, well let freckle-face give them out.' And he goes out in a ferocious temper, slamming the door behind him.

Now listen to me, mother, before punishing that poor boy. He has behaved badly, true enough. But we must admit he controlled himself to some extent, because when we saw freckle-face appear, we all thought he would just cram the sweets into his mouth and keep chewing until there were none left. He deserves some punishment. But you must understand that it was your fault; that is no way to teach a child to be generous.

A MOTHER AND AN ANGEL

> *The little ones prayed thus: 'Holy Mary, Mother of God, play with us, sinners . . . ' What else could the Blessed Virgin do but play with those little three-year-olds?*

You must live a united life in the home: always united, enjoying yourselves together, suffering together, praying together. In a Christian home that is truly alive, there must be prayer in common. 'Prayer in common has more effect on the heart of God', said Pope Pius XII.

'Where two or three are gathered together in my name, I am there in the midst of them' (Matthew 18, 20).

Together, parents and children, always united in the sight of the Lord, in your own house and in the house of your Father God.

In the middle of your work towards the end of the morning, at twelve o'clock, when the mother is still putting the house in order, and the children are jumping and playing about, and the father is beginning to feel tired with the day's work, again you will be united spiritually as you all say the *Angelus* to the Mother of God. You will receive great encouragement when you recall the Archangel's greeting and Mary's generous reply. Her 'Be it done unto me' will help us all to renew the task with greater effort. You will both pray for each other and for the children, who are probably jumping around the house at that moment. Teach the little ones to speak to their Lady.

'In the name of our Lord we beg you', says Pius XII, 'to do everything to preserve intact the beautiful Christian family tradition of reciting evening prayers together, in order to implore God's blessing and to honour the Immaculate Virgin of the Rosary with her praises, having gathered together the entire household at each day's end. In the beginning, just the two of you; then . . . the little ones whom providence shall entrust to you, and also those whom our Lord has placed at your side.'

Anyone who lives his divine filiation and realises that he is a child of God cannot but acknowledge that he received life anew through a Virgin who was faithful to the word of God. How then can he possibly cease to pray to his Mother, both individually and collectively?

Yes, say the family Rosary, without hurrying; do not let the children pray at such a speed as would suggest that they do not really want to be understood. Do things properly. The holy Rosary cannot be allowed to degenerate into a monotonous sing-song. Recite it as it should be recited.

The very young should say only one mystery. And doubtless even then you will have to stop at about the fifth Hail Mary to remind them that they are speaking to their Mother in heaven. From her throne, she presides over the home and watches over you all throughout the day. It would be so easy for us to pay her many little compliments and say nice things to her, if only we wanted to! So, teach your children to look at her and to salute her at least whenever they enter or leave the house.

Pray to Mary that your children may grow up with a great devotion to her, for that is a sure pledge of salvation.

Spiritual books have always related many wonders attributed to the Blessed Virgin. And if you will allow me, I too will tell you something about her.

You can tell your children that a friend of yours was present when this happened. I was . . . well, never mind where; it is better that I don't say too much. I was called out urgently; a dying man was calling for a priest, any priest to come quickly. So I went.

At first I was not allowed to enter the house. No priest had ever gone in there, and I was regarded with suspicion and hostility. But Mary overcame all that, and I managed to get in.

I want to tell you this in detail. The same thing happened in that house as in the stories you read about. There was a man in the bed, breathing his last. I shall never forget it, for I was deeply moved, and the big man who lay there dying was just as touched as I was. His confession was very difficult, I could scarcely hear him. I had to put my ear to his lips. It was a long confession, and when he had finished – he had only a few minutes to live – he wanted to tell me about his 'miracle'. He did so panting, absolutely exhausted. I thanked him with all my heart.

He had been away from the Church for forty years.

'You will be wondering why I called for a priest.'

I said nothing; he did all the talking.

'When my mother was dying' – now it was almost impossible to hear him – 'she called us all together, her children. "Look", she said, "I have nothing to leave you. But do what I tell you now. Say three Hail Marys every night." And I did that' – the poor man was weeping aloud – 'I did that, you see, I did that.'

He died while speaking. That was all like a wonderful hymn to me: 'I did that. I did that.'

There you have what I wanted to tell you. It is just like the stories told in those religious books, but it is a true story that ended with the salvation of that soul. And I made a resolution to tell it whenever I could. So now I too can say 'I did that.'

> *You see the value of having a Mother like Mary in heaven!*
> *Every man in the world will do great courtesy*
> *Who gives his service to the Virgin Mary.*
> *While alive, he will know happiness*
> *And will save his soul at the last day.*
> *(Gonzalo de Berceo)*

I have no intention of dictating the acts of piety that should be practised in your family. But in various parts of this book, such as the following paragraphs, I do mention some pious practices, in order simply to suggest to you some of the many good things you can do. It is up to you, remembering also what you yourself saw done in your own family, to try and form in your children a solid, doctrinal and practical piety, so that they may always keep alive their sense of being children of God, of their divine filiation.

How grateful the Lord will surely be to you if your children remember, when they are grown up, something we all remember from our young days: that the month of May has always been the month devoted to our Lady, the month of flowers. And how pleasing it must be for him to see a whole family, parents and children, go to one of her shrines in May and say the Rosary there.

Another thing your children should be taught very young is that they should prepare for the great feast of the Immaculate Conception by making a joyful novena.

From an early age they should also get used to the sacramental of sprinkling Holy Water before going to bed, to wipe out all the venial sins they have committed during the day.

None of this will be difficult, for you have the angels helping you. Teach them that there are angels for each one of us, angels who offer our prayers to God, who are with us in trouble and in joy, who rejoice when we are happy, who help us to avoid temptations. And you yourself must often remember your child's Guardian Angel, for each person has one. You, mother, who complain so much that you have to stay all alone in the house with the baby, you forget that there are four of you there. You, your child, your angel and his.

God has planned things very well. He has given each child a father, a mother and an angel to protect him.

Get into the habit of saluting your Guardian Angel often: don't grow out of Angels as you grow out of Santa Claus.

NOT EVERYTHING IS SINFUL

As I already said, you must teach your children to have a solid and doctrinal piety. So they should learn their Catechism perfectly. That means you must know it yourself.

You should not regard the study of our religion as in the same category as the study of numismatics. The amount of religious ignorance we find nowadays is amazing. 'Hear the word of the Lord, ye children of Israel: for the Lord shall enter into judgment with the inhabitants of the land. For there is no truth, and there is no mercy, and there is no knowledge of God in the land' (Osee 4, 1). Make every effort to form them well in the Catechism of their Christian doctrine.

The religious knowledge they learn must take a positive form. 'If you tell lies, the devil will take you away' is the type of thing you should never say, because it is simply not true. When speaking to your children, omit from your vocabulary such phrases as: God will punish you, you will go to hell, that is a serious sin. Would you yourself really want to send your children to hell for such little misdeeds as they do? Well then, remember that God is their Father too.

Do not joke on a cold day about hell being a warm place, for hell is much too serious a reality for that kind of thing. And do not describe heaven as a static, motionless or boring place. You often seem to associate the idea of being good with the idea of being quiet. 'Stay quiet and be good' is a phrase that children hate; they want action simply because, thanks be to God, they are normal and healthy. That horrible phrase annoyed one poor child so much that he asked: 'Mummy, in heaven will we have to be good too?'

Do not describe the devil as you would describe witches, fairies or ghosts. Make no comparisons between fact and fiction, history and legend. Whatever else you do, avoid all ridiculous superstitions and silly scruples.

It is only natural that the 'adult' God of the grown-ups should be a Child God for children, in keeping with their mentality, but make sure he is a Child as Jesus really was. I mention this because I was horrified by a question that a child once asked me: 'Was Jesus a little boy or a little girl?' And he showed me a picture of the Child Jesus at school with a most unboyish face. 'He was a boy' I answered sharply, tearing up that picture.

Here is a story of an intelligent father. He and his son are in the Church. Just before the time for Holy Communion he notices that his son looks worried.

'Daddy, I have committed a sin. I cannot receive Holy Communion.'

The father knows his son and tries to console him.

'What have you done, son?'

'You remember the pen you gave me; well, I sold it.'

The father with great affection and wisdom says:

'How much did you get for it?'

Looking his father in the eye, and now very sorry, he whispers: 'Ninepence.'

The father takes him out of his seat and says:

'Come on to Holy Communion. That wasn't a sin, that was only a bad bargain.'

YOU ARE NOT SPIRITUAL DIRECTORS

Prayer in common and union of hearts, yes, but . . . there always seem to be 'buts'. The 'but' in this case is called discretion. You have to be a good husband to your wife, but not a spiritual director; nor you, to your husband. Neither of you has been given the grace of state necessary for that.

Who told you you should demand an account from your wife at the time of her examination of conscience? Examine your own faults and ask God to forgive them. Your wife will make her own examination and ask forgiveness for her failures. Each of you should ask pardon for your own sins and the sins of your children. And be discreet because, as Pope Pius XII said, 'a husband and wife are not confessors.'

Never try to intrude on another's conscience, not even under the mistaken pretext of apostolate. Do not pry into another's interior life. This would be completely misguided zeal. I know husbands who are actually envious of the spiritual progress made by their wives. I saw those same men some time ago, advising their wives on how to improve their interior life. Then later on, when they did increase in the love of God, the husbands felt they had been left behind.

Believe me, the role of spiritual director is most unsuited to you. Leave that task to those entrusted with it by the Church. Be discreet and you will remain perfectly united with one another. And if it should happen, which God forbid, that you find you are directed to do something against the precepts of divine law, 'then preserve and defend respectfully, quietly, affectionately, but firmly and unshakeably, all the inalienable and sacred independence of your own conscience' (Pius XII).

SPEAKING OF GOD

Parents, do not spend all day speaking about God, for Pope Pius XII says: 'There is no need to speak constantly of God.'

If you live your divine filiation, if you realise that you are children of God, if your relationship with him, as with a Father, is based on confidence, then your children will grow up in those surroundings, in that atmosphere, where all the supernatural realities and truths are lived in a natural way. And that is the important thing. If our life and our death are left in the hands of the Lord, then no difficulties, no doubts, no shocks will frighten us. 'It is I, fear not', says the good Father who looks after us in every difficulty. You will 'take everything that happens to thee as good, knowing that nothing happens without God' (*The Didache*).

Here again I must remind you that the most important thing is for your home to be really alive. Make sure that your children's consciences are properly formed: Christ is not a little boy with golden curls and a pink dress; nor is he a child that performs miracles while playing with his friends; nor a tyrant waiting around the corner to pounce on human weaknesses and punish the offenders; nor a powerful businessman with whom we can make bargains.

God is our Father, because he has made us his children; he is our Friend, because he has called us his friends; he is our Brother, who gave his life for all; he is Love asking for love and generosity in return; he is the Almighty, who has reserved for us in heaven the happiest home imaginable for all eternity.

Living homes; yes, but to form living homes involves one great difficulty. It demands that you teach your children about God primarily and mainly by means of your own life. It is no use going into raptures telling them how good God is, if they see afterwards that you do not approach him as frequently as you preach. They are watching you.

Perhaps you would like me to show you some other system of teaching, that would be less demanding and leave the parents more scope to do as they wish. But it does not exist! Perhaps you would like to think that the school should be able to educate them in spite of the fact that you yourselves do not live as you should. No, the school has no magic formula to form your children. They will live as you live. So you will have only yourselves to blame afterwards. Christian education of children demands that the parents should live lives face to face with Christ always.

The great transformation which Christianity has to bring to the world is already alive in the homes of Christ's followers, ready to penetrate later into society, into every sector of society, into every aspect of human activity. Your children will either form part of the lifeless mass, the heap of moving bodies that walk about our streets, or else they will join the throng of living men who have risen and accepted Life. They will live as they see you live.

2

CHRISTIAN HOMES

DO NO WRONG!

> *'I have the fear that . . . there will be dissension, rivalry, ill humour, factiousness, backbiting, gossip, self-conceit, disharmony among you . . . that I shall have to shed tears over many of you': these are words of Saint Paul to the Corinthians.*

I doubt that, in reading these cold printed words, you will get any idea of the swift, vigorous, enormous strokes with which I am starting to write this page.

I have just come in from the street. I have actually run up the stairs to begin writing – shouting – to you a few loud words: teach your children that they must never harm anyone in any way! Even in the street you see them doing so much harm to one another!

Teach them – and you are responsible if they do not learn it – that we Christians cannot harm our fellow men. What do people think love means, anyway?

'Be attentive to me and hear me; I am grieved in my exercise and am troubled . . . For if my enemy had reviled me, I would verily have borne with it. And if he that hated me had spoken great things against me, I would perhaps have hidden myself from him. But thou, a man of one mind with me, my guide, my familiar, who didst take sweet meats together with me: in the house of God we walked with consent . . . He hath stretched forth his hand to repay. They have defiled his covenant. They are divided by the wrath of his countenance, and his heart hath drawn near. His words are smoother than oil: and

the same are darts . . . Bloody and deceitful men shall
not live out half their days: but I will trust in thee, O
Lord' (Psalm 54).

Today I am the victim, tomorrow it will be you. The
envious never rest.

'By the envy of the devil, death came into the world:
and they that are of his side follow him' (Wisdom 2, 24-
25).

There are many followers of the devil going about the
world, trying to destroy the happiness of united Christian homes. You can be quite sure that when, by the
grace of God and by your own efforts, your home becomes what you and I want it to be – a home full of light
and joy, peace and happiness – you will find yourself
again carrying the cross, a burning cross placed on your
shoulders by the envious. I have seen them at work and
I can tell you about it.

Once upon a time – I begin as if this were a short fairy
story, but in fact it is long and only too true – there was
a large family. It was a deeply Christian family in which
the children, already strong in spite of their tender years,
loved one another immensely. It was a fortress of hearts
united around the father and mother. Their love was as
Christ wants it to be: each one forgetting himself and
thinking only of the others, for they had all learned, by
that blessed infection, to make life more pleasant for
the others. It was a happy home. Each one did his work
with ambition and enthusiasm, because each one felt
responsible for making the house as it should be by the
united efforts of all.

But then came those people who are saddened to see
others trying to do good, and who suffer when they see
good men yield fruit or be successful.

These people – and every little village has its share of
them – tried to do something that only the imagination
of loathsome devils could think up. They tried to break

down the unity between the mother and father. And slander is so very powerful! They wanted to break up that love which united the children so closely. To see peace reigning in that Christian family was like a burning fire in the cruel hearts of the envious, those friends of unholy war.

The hour of suffering came to that home. It was another case of the Lord allowing his followers to taste the bitterness of the cross, before tasting again the sweetness of his peace and joy.

It was the father himself who told me this, after the storm had blown over and all the slander had been destroyed by the power of the Lord. His words made me weep, for I was not accustomed to seeing so much evil. And I wept all the more when, with the serenity of a saint, he repeated to me a few phrases which I knew by heart: 'In your apostolic undertaking don't fear the enemies "outside", however great their power. This is the enemy most to be feared: your lack of "filiation" and your lack of "fraternal" spirit' (*The Way*, 955)

It may seem strange that we Christians should still have to be reminded that we must not harm others. But in fact we do. And this is a fundamental and most important point. You will have opportunities later on to teach your children that they should love their enemies, but for the moment I would prefer you to tell them this, which is so elementary: not to harm others.

Sometimes I wonder if we should not organise a society for the prevention of cruelty to humans, where people could come to take refuge from lashing tongues, slanders, defamations and all kinds of destructive criticism.

Do not speak badly of others. You who go frequently to Holy Communion, to receive Love itself, try to understand the meaning of that charity which God demands of us; be careful not to limit its definition to giving a few coins to the poor.

The most common failing among 'good people' is gossip. You are always speaking about people, what they said and did. On your tongue there is always someone's name, and always a little bit of spite or malice. You pour out damaging words as you would let water run through your fingers, and you never seem to stop and think how far your gossip goes. That 'bit of news' that escaped from your lips is now being repeated again and again amid sneers and laughter, and as it is passed along recklessly it destroys the merits, the honour and the hearts of the people concerned; it sows the seeds of pessimism and poisons all joy. Finally it will come to an end, of course . . . when it dies down at the frontier of eternity. But by then that little 'opinion' of yours – for that is what you call your slanderous gossip – after careering along wildly from mouth to mouth, will be exhausted, twisted, torn, with tatters of human flesh hanging from it, bits of honour and merit now frayed and utterly destroyed, scraps of happiness and joy that once were real. And those are the trophies that will await you when you pass through the gates to your eternity!

Harm no one: let that simple idea be the subject of many discussions with your children. 'Offend no man, neither the small nor the great' (Ecclesiasticus 5, 18). 'How shall I curse him, whom God hath not cursed?' (Numbers 23, 8).

Little by little get them to realise that there are other children who have their own ambitions, and with just as much right to have them as they themselves. And they must never try to thwart the ambitions of others. Get them to understand that there are many other people in the world besides themselves, each one with a perfect right to live, to think and to work. They must respect the honour, the good name and the freedom of their fellow men.

You must speak to them of sanctity and tell them that their greatest ambition must be to achieve it, but explain to them in a practical way that there can be no possible sanctity without service of one's neighbour. And the great obstacle to love and service of our neighbour is envy. The streets are thronged with envious people, hearts who feel sad to see others happy! Those, and only those, will be happy who seek all their joy in making life pleasant, enjoyable, cheerful and happy for others.

Nature itself has placed in the hearts of all men an impulse, a natural tendency to love others. Do not quench it. 'Take care that you stress what characterises our quality of children of God, namely: the unity of life which links the Christian with God and with his brothers. Nothing should break, or even disturb, that spiritual union which is based on love, the necessary condition of which is the peace of man with God and the harmony of men among themselves' (Chevrot).

Yes, we must all be better than we are. Each one of us must say: 'I have to improve', and then do so. Look: if each one swept in front of his own door, the whole street would be clean. So let us try and see what needs to be done in our home.

The first duty you have towards your children is that you two should love each other very much, as much as you did before you were married. That is the first thing you have to do. Do you think you can create a good home atmosphere simply by preaching sermons on love? With those little eyes that pry into everything, the children will see the affection or disunion, the joy or discord, that exists between you. They will love you and will love one another very much if you love each other as you should.

Children are always able to forgive their father or mother the mistakes they make in trivial unimportant things, but they cannot understand disunity or disagreement on the great principles regulating the home.

I think this passage from Tagore is relevant here; it has certainly given me cause for reflection and perhaps it may also give you some food for thought. These are words of the Bengali poet on his return to India after travelling through Christian countries:

'If you, Christians, lived like Christ, the whole of India would be at your feet . . . Master Jesus, there is no place for you in Europe. Come, find a place among us, in Asia, in the country of Buddha. Our hearts are filled with sadness and your coming will comfort them.'

MAKING YOUR FRIENDS HAPPY

> *'Where are there people so brutish as not to love one another when they live together and are continually in one another's company . . . and believe that God loves us and that they themselves love God?' (Saint Teresa of Avila)*

Christian parents, it is your duty to form Christian homes where that charity will be lived fully which Christ preaches to us today, from the Gospel.

There is a whole educational programme implied in that principle of merely not harming others, but nevertheless you must not allow yourselves to be content with those negative lessons of love. You will be approaching the ideal when the efforts of each member of your family are aimed at making the others happy.

Some years ago during the Christmas holidays I took a group of boys to a priest's house, and each boy brought along some present or other. This priest had organised a Christmas party and would give out the presents to those children whom Santa Claus did not visit because they were very poor. One of the boys who came with me was very sad-looking because he had wanted to give his latest model train, but his mother at the last moment – such was her generosity! – had sent instead an old ragged doll. I remember that good priest taking the presents and thanking the boys, with these words that really touched their hearts: 'I thank you very sincerely, because with these toys of yours you are going to make many other children happy.'

To make a child happy! To make life easier for someone in need! In this alone there is a whole programme of sanctification through joy, but that is something which the woman who replaced the train by the old torn doll could never understand.

To become a saint by making life more pleasant for others: I spoke to you about that some years ago in my first book, but I have no hesitation in coming back to it again, because you need it. Parents, this is how you will merit heaven, the heaven of eternity and also the heaven of your home.

Do not unburden your troubles to your family. On the contrary, let your shoulders bear the weight of theirs. 'There is no irritating thing that is not easily got over in those who love one another, and it must be a grave thing if it does annoy' (Saint Teresa).

Be careful not to let your house be filled with bad humour; no angry scenes; no outbursts of rage; no fits of temper; no quick answers; no hurtful words. Your family must not become the victims of the hard blows you receive from others in the street, in the office or at the counter.

They must be able to rely on you always, even when you are in bad humour! I do understand your strong temperament, but I cannot see why you make the effort to control it in front of strangers, people who mean nothing to you, and then let it overcome you completely, brutally and stupidly when you are alone with your own family. Those nearest to you should come first.

To speak to your children about the sufferings of the pagan children in Africa and not to tell them anything about the sufferings of those closer to you is quite unchristian, in the same way as it is a bad educational method to make a town boy learn by heart the names of the mountains and rivers of Africa if he has never seen a river or a mountain in his life. Explorations and charity should both begin with what is nearest to them.

Parents, no selfishness: or your children will he infected with it. No petty bargaining, or they will grow up to be very mean. No negative criticism, or they will want to control everything themselves. No misunderstandings, or you will make them miserable.

Sow the seeds of mutual affection in your home, and your children will love God with all their heart, with all their mind, with all their soul, with all their strength . . . by loving their neighbour.

SERVING OTHERS

Everyone who is incorporated in Christ must regard himself and the whole of his life as at the service of men. 'The Christian', says Schmaus, 'does not direct his cultural or political efforts to producing objective values, but to producing values for the welfare and use of man. Saint Augustine says that earthly power is a function of service.' That is what I want to speak to you about now: this spirit of service which must inspire your life and the lives of those around you.

Your own life, first of all. Your children must see with their own eyes how they are to give themselves to others. When they see how you behave within the family they must understand that love in this life consists of doing good deeds.

You have a grave responsibility to keep alive that same spirit lived by the first generations of Christians. From these two passages by Athenagoras you can see the tone of the lives lived by those men: 'We base our religion, not on making speeches, but on teaching and giving example by deeds.' 'Among us you might find simple folk, artisans and old women who, although they may be incapable of expressing in words the assistance they derive from our doctrine, yet show in their deeds the advantage to others that accrues from their resolution. They do not rehearse words but show forth good deeds; they do not strike back those who strike them, they do not take to justice those who do them injustice, to them that ask they give, and they love their neighbour as themselves.' These two passages contain all I want to tell you.

There are so many topics you can bring up to chat about with your children in a friendly way!

Little by little you should explain the meaning of the Gospel to them. There you have a wonderful family apostolate. Try to show them how the affection Christ had for his followers made him wash the dirty feet of his disciples.

Get them to develop a spirit of serving others and teach them what that embraces: a spirit of sacrifice. And there you have the foundation for all that social formation, which is so necessary nowadays.

If you fail to do that, they will grow up to be individualists in the bad sense of the word, comfort-seekers, with miserly souls: unless they have the right background, they will be frightened when they are told of the concern they must have for all the problems, needs, interests, rights, tastes and lives of others. We cannot allow generations of men exclusively devoted to their own affairs to grow up in our homes. We must do everything possible to train them in generosity.

If God is love – as he is – then man, made in the image and likeness of God, must be the same. And love thinks only of others; it is a very sad and selfish love otherwise. Love becomes real in giving to others.

However paradoxical it may seem, I must tell you, with Schmaus, that man becomes fully developed, fully realised, only when he gives himself to others, when he sacrifices himself. Does that appear strange to you? Well, open the Gospel: 'He who keeps his life will lose it, and he who loses his life will keep it.'

We must give ourselves; you must give yourselves; I must give myself. That is the only way we can teach others that they must give themselves.

And when they ask you to explain the meaning of sacrifice, of giving oneself to God by giving oneself to one's brothers, one's friends, one's neighbours, you can tell them how God himself clearly explained to Saul in the midst of dazzling light after knocking him from his horse, this very lesson that your children must learn. On the way to Damascus Saul learned and understood for the first time that to persecute a few men who were called Christians was to persecute Jesus himself. From then on, in the background of all Saint Paul's letters, like a refrain that appears again and again in all kinds of contexts, you find that idea: whatever we do to other men, we do to Christ.

It is never too soon to begin to teach your children this spirit of service, this sense of sacrificing themselves for others, as the seed-bed in which their sense of social responsibility is to grow.

If you really want your children to grow up with this spirit of serving others, teach them that all the talents they have received from God (intelligence, memory, will-power, strength, spirit of initiative, spirit of hard work, loyalty, and all the human and supernatural virtues) have a social function. They have received them all from

God to be placed at the disposal of their neighbour. Their money, too, their goods and all their great ideals.

If you want your children to cultivate this spirit of service, teach them always to respect the rights, the opinions and the property of others. In your family life for instance, do not allow anyone to humiliate or make jokes at the expense of another.

Try to find out whether your child is a good friend, whether he is sincere and loyal to his companions. Find out whether he has learned to lend his toys, his notes, his books and pencils to his schoolmates, or whether he is becoming selfish and miserly with those notes, books, or coloured pencils.

There is a danger that any son may turn out to be like the prodigal; but there is a much greater danger that he may become like the prodigal's brother: mean, miserly and gloomy to see the joy caused by his brother's return. While the angels are rejoicing over the conversion of a sinner who does penance, the prodigal's brother becomes sad.

Have no doubt whatever but that the proper reaction is in that joy of the angels, in your joy and mine.

Like the apostles on one occasion and like the brother of the prodigal son, your children may easily adopt a wrong attitude towards sinners, people who are devoted to pleasure and have gone astray. That is what you are there for: to correct and admonish, always in a tactful way, as Christ did, as the father of the prodigal son did.

The apostles wanted to call down fire and brimstone on the proud cities, and the selfish brother complained about the banquet organised to celebrate the return of the prodigal. But on those occasions Christ gives doctrine and the good father reprimands his faithful son.

SOCIAL DUTIES

If you want them to practise a spirit of service, a sense of social responsibility, then explain to them that hundreds and thousands of men of all races and in all parts of the world cooperate in manufacturing our food and our clothes; tell them about the work that many workers had to do, so that they could have their breakfast comfortably when they got up that morning; describe something of the sacrifices that the miners have to make in order to obtain light and heat for them from the bowels of the earth.

If they understand those things, then you can be sure that a great affection, sympathy and gratitude will begin to make themselves felt in them towards the workers, those older brothers of theirs, and you will have to speak to them very little about social reforms. 'Children who have been brought up in the spirit which we have just outlined, when they reach an adult age, will know themselves that they must oppose class selfishness, whether it comes from above or below, in every social conflict' (Foerster).

Are you beginning to realise now all the things that you can do with your children?

And from there, from those material things, it will be easy to pass on and explain to them the Communion of Saints. There are certain social duties which must he carried out unfailingly by every Christian, for they are at the very centre of Christianity. The Church is a juridical community and at the same time it is the Mystical Body of Christ, a living reality, composed of many members, all of whom need one another.

One thing you must never do, unless you want your children to become useless both to God and to society, is something that was done by one poor mother – I mean poor in her knowledge of what God demands of us regarding the spirit of service and of love. When this woman heard that on the school outings all the sandwiches were mixed together and given out indiscriminately to everyone during the meal, so that everyone got some of what the others had brought, she told her child in a determined tone: 'From now on when you go on the outings, I'll give you no more ham – for all the others to eat.' Poor child! What is he to think in his little mind when that same mother begins to teach him – by word only, of course – about love of God and of his neighbour?

For God's sake, give them none of those hackneyed lectures on the importance of looking after themselves above all else. That type of pedagogy belongs to the time of the Renaissance, and we are in the twentieth century now. What your children need is good team work on all levels. You tell them far too often that charity begins at home; but you do not understand this phrase yourselves. Charity does not mean giving in to their own little likes and dislikes. What you should tell them is that the likes and dislikes of others must come before their own.

The first time your child says the Hail Mary aloud, when he comes to 'pray for us, sinners', explain to him who 'us' are: his father, his mother, brothers and sisters, workers, friends, teachers, priests, all those he does not know and also those who are called 'bad people'. In that word 'us', all men are included, because we all make up one single Body.

And make sure that, when he takes his toys out to play with other children, he still remembers who are included in that 'us'.

At an early age, as soon as they learn to say 'what is mine is mine', make them aware of misery, of slums, of those poor wretches who sleep in the parks, and of children who are hungry.

And when your children are older, make sure that they become quite familiar with the life and problems of sick and handicapped people. Let them visit a hospital from time to time. Perhaps this advice will surprise you. But they must learn from an early age that the word 'us' also includes those who suffer.

ALMS

> Here is how the first Christians lived: 'If there is among them any that is poor and needy, and if they have no spare food, they fast two or three days in order to supply to the needy their lack of food' (Aristides).

When we say that everything of value and all the virtues that you and your children have are to be used also for the benefit of others, we must not exclude money from this principle. Our money too has to fulfil a function other than satisfying our own needs. Later on I shall speak to you about the pocket-money which your children ask for and you give them every so often. For the moment I am still referring to the meaning of 'us' in the Hail Mary.

This 'us' also includes the poor, those who are often called nowadays by other better-sounding names, but who are still poor. The early Christians knew the Holy Scripture; they knew that they had to help the poor. 'If one of thee brethren that dwelleth within the gates of thy city in the land which the Lord thy God will give thee come to poverty, thou shalt not harden thy heart, nor close thy hand, but shalt open it to the poor man . . . Thou shalt give to him. Neither shalt thou do any thing craftily in relieving his necessities: that the Lord thy God may bless thee at all times, and in all things to which thou shalt put thy hand. There will not be wanting poor in the land . . . therefore I command thee to open thy hand to thy needy and poor brother, that liveth in the land' (Deuteronomy 15, 7-11).

The early Christians knew the doctrine of Christ and they put it into practice. 'We who once loved money above all things and the increase of our goods, now even what little we have we use in common, and from it we give a share to everyone who is in need' (Saint Justin). 'When you can do good, defer it not, because "alms deliver from death"' (Saint Polycarp). 'It is obvious and undeniable . . . that it is a good thing to visit . . . the poor with many children' (Saint Clement). Among the early Christians even the poor gave, at great cost to themselves: 'If there is among them any that is poor and needy, and if they have no spare food, they fast two or three days in order to supply to the needy their lack of food' (Aristides).

We must agree that they lived their Christianity more sincerely than we do. Nowadays, when it comes to having children or to giving alms, we all hide and shelter behind the shield which bears the motto: 'The others have no children, the others give nothing'. We are in danger of bringing up a generation of people who do not even know the meaning of the word alms.

You say you do give alms? Yes, you give cents and nickels. So many people give nickels to the poor and to the Church. And these are rewarded certainly, but only when the giver has very little money, as in the case of the poor widow in the Gospel. You put your hand in your trouser pocket only for the Church and for the poor, because that is where you keep your small change. Is that how you think you will build up a store of treasure in heaven? Where did you learn that type of generosity? Like the Pharisees, you want to fulfil the letter of the Gospel and so you give, at most, a glass of cold water, but with no love of God.

What will your children learn of alms-giving from watching you? In years to come, when the nickel is no longer in circulation, what will they give?

Cents and nickels; keep on giving your cents and nickels! Do you think, sincerely, that many problems will be solved or great apostolates carried out by the Church with those cents and nickles you give? When attendants need change for their tills they go to the sacristy nearby, because there they are sure to find the cents they want. What would Saint Paul say to you today if he were going from house to house collecting alms? Just think how many of the great apostolic undertakings that have already been begun could be finished if you helped financially. It might be interesting to add up the sum total of the alms you gave to the Church and the poor last year. You would add it up very quickly because it would be very easy, if you decided not to count the cents and nickles.

But you must not count that bonus you gave your employees at Christmas as charity. Remember you gave them that extra only because you knew they would tear the place down otherwise. It comes under the heading not of 'charity' but of 'insurance'. Yes, those workers are very annoying when they begin to grumble! Don't you think 'the priests' should try and teach them to accept their fate with 'Christian resignation'?

I have seen the poor widow mentioned in the Gospel – and you can tell your children this. I know now how Jesus' eyes lit up when he saw her place two mites, all the money she had, in the temple collection-box. The woman I have seen is seventy five, very wrinkled and bent almost double; she suffers very much but is always cheerful. She is one of those old women who go to Church very early every morning. She knows nothing of those percentage rules some people use to regulate the alms they give, so she has invented her own rules. She has a small weekly income, of which she spends half on herself and, as she has no children, she gives the other half away to the poor. I must admit that she has one kind of passion, but it is a holy passion: that no one should know. What a blessed passion, and what a blessed old woman! She has truly learned what Christ teaches in the Gospel.

The rule for alms-giving invented by her is a flexible one. Here in her own words is another of the points in her rule: 'Last week, instead of spending all my allowance, I managed to save a bit, so this week I'll be able to give them a little more.' And she took several banknotes out of an old purse; these were her savings over the year. And she will continue to give those alms every week until she dies. She will have nothing left on this earth . . . But she is quite sure – just as you and I are sure – that she is filling a big purse in the kingdom of heaven.

That old woman does not know that I have written a little chapter of her life in this book. When it is printed, that good woman, already bent double and suffering immensely but without ever losing her good humour, may already be in heaven and have found an old purse filled with grains of gold.

That good woman learned to give and to give herself, many years ago in her parents' home, watching what they did. Will your children learn the meaning of alms, of charity, in the same way?

REST AND RECREATION

> *You may well be the mother of that boy who complained to me: 'I never see my mother because she is always out giving lectures on how to educate children.'*

Six pairs of apostles, with neither food nor money, went about teaching and curing the children of Israel, carrying out a command from Jesus. Judas also anointed the sick and cured them. So the twelve apostles, going about in groups, gave health to lepers and life to the dead. Those were days of unceasing toil, of continuous but joyful work.

On their return they went to the Lord and told him all they had done and taught. When he saw how tired they were, Jesus said to them: 'Come away into a quiet place by yourselves, and rest a little' because, Saint Mark tells us, 'there were many coming and going, and they scarcely had leisure even to eat.' So they took the boat and returned to Bethsaida.

Rest is necessary. Work is certainly a duty, but it is neither the only one nor even the most important.

I know many parents who are quite happy with themselves because they work hard. They have what they like to call a passion for work, although in some cases it is rather a passion for money. I must tell those parents that any occupation which takes up every hour in the day of a father of a family is not carried out in a Christian way.

Your work is not Christian if it keeps you from attending to God, your wife, your children or your friends. By this I mean that, in your plan of life, there must be a time set apart, not only for your work, but also for God and for your recreation and rest, which does not mean doing nothing (cf *The Way*, 357), but attending to your family and the apostolate.

Jesus was sitting down chatting to his friends when some mothers came to him with their children and asked him to bless them. He looked at the children smiling, but the impulsive disciples pushed them aside so as not to annoy their Master. And Jesus had to restrain and admonish those tough fishermen: 'Suffer the little children to come to me . . . ' And they began to play around him while he blessed them.

Think of all the things Lazarus, Martha and Mary could tell us about their 'get-togethers' with Jesus! Did you think he never rested? Of course he did; what he never did was to waste time, which is different.

We could also learn many interesting things about Jesus' rest from his meeting with the Samaritan woman at Jacob's well (John 4, 6-42); Chevrot has written a whole book about that passage.

When your children come home from school, none of them could tell such wonderful stories as the apostles were telling Jesus in that chat of theirs when they were interrupted by the multitude who came along, hungry for bread and for doctrine. Your children cannot tell you about casting out devils or about curing paralytics. They can only tell you what they have done and learned that day. But they will come home to you after school with the very same joy as those twelve. They were coming back to Jesus, and your children are coming back to their father and mother. It is true they will have nothing of transcendental importance to speak about, only little escapades and stories; but at the time of those get-togethers with your children your home can have the same charm as the conversation between Jesus and his apostles.

Some days you will find them – again just like the apostles – fighting for the privilege of sitting beside their father. In these things neither good manners nor brotherly affection are strong enough to give way to rights of birth. On that occasion the Lord had to intervene and correct them, as you also will have to do. But there is no need to worry. Little desires for revenge, certain ignoble ambitions, pride, vanity, human outlook: these are some of the defects we find in the apostles. So you cannot be surprised to find them also in your children.

Jesus related sublime truths about love. You will have to be content with lesser things, within the understanding of young intelligences. Children have a right to recreation and rest with their parents within the home, and parents have a duty to rest with their children. 'Good,

Mummy: tomorrow we'll be together all day, from morning till night', said a little lad of six the day before setting out on a long train journey.

Mothers, especially, make sure you understand the importance of this. It would be very bad if they were with you only on holidays. That would be intolerable; there could be no excuse for it – you running around to all sorts of places while the children are at home waiting for you.

Mothers, what are you doing away from home every evening? If your absence is necessary, God will certainly make up for it; but if you are simply enjoying yourselves, then your absence becomes a vice, a vice that will end up by destroying the family.

You ask me how you are to find time to be with them. But that question is asked in the wrong way; because remember: the first and most important things on this earth for you are your husband and your children. After that, you can begin to ask how you are to find time to do other things outside the home.

Had you thought, for a moment, that your social obligations were more important than the time devoted to your children? You think you have to go out every night. But, tell me, who commands you to do that? You cannot let anyone or anything lord it over you like that.

You say you cannot be at home when the children return from school. Well, what a pity! You say they see you only on holidays. In that case, accuse yourselves seriously of neglecting your duties as parents.

The get-together I have been speaking about is a cheerful daily reunion where all the members of the family tell of the incidents and the little adventures of the day; where the father and mother tell the family history; where everyone forgets the cold and the troubles of the world outside. It is a reunion where everyone learns to do little things to help the others. The get-together should always be packed with little acts of thoughtfulness.

It is not the time to examine the lessons, but simply to be a friend to your children. In the get-together the children learn to love, to be mad about their parents, like Lazarus' sister when she was sitting at the feet of the Lord. It is the time when the parents and children play together, tell stories, sing songs, laugh, and everyone is in good humour; it is the blessed hour of family rest and recreation. 'Thy children as olive plants, round about the table' (Psalm 127).

LOVE AMONG GYPSY CHILDREN

Do you genuinely want to know the meaning of affection? Do you genuinely want to live a life of unity among parents and children in your home? Then you must learn the true meaning of love. And you can learn that now from a couple of gypsy children. We all need to be reminded of how to love, and we are going to get a reminder from these youngsters. The story I am going to tell you will be of equal benefit to parents and to children.

We are looking at Puerta Elvira, with its thirteen battlements. We go past it now, turn to the right, and here we are at the scene of the story. It is a scene still bathed in light, just as it was then. All the sun of Andalusia was shining on the slope of Alhacaba, the hill leading up to the Albaycin district in Granada. Here on the left, the same stream was flowing, with the same water. Now look higher up. It was on the right of that house you see in front of you that the two little gypsies appeared. And these are the pot-bellied heroes of our story, brought into this world by poor parents who loved children.

The smaller one was very happy and clapping his hands. His trimmed curly hair was falling onto his forehead. His little shirt only half covered him. He was almost black, a kind of dusty grey-black, like the dust of the road. He walked in bare feet on the sharp gravel on the path. He cannot have been more than about five years old. The bigger of the two must have been about ten.

The bits of clothes worn by the two brothers would have been about sufficient to cover one of them fully. The little one had half a shirt, and the big one had trousers that were kept up by a string hanging over one black shoulder, black like blackened wood. The little one was dancing round his brother, who emerged slowly and solemnly with a bottle of milk from the house on the right. Then he began to speak

'Sit down. I'll drink first and then you'll drink.'

If only you could have heard him! He spoke like an emperor. The younger one was looking up at him, showing his white teeth, his mouth half open and the tip of his tongue sticking out.

And I was there fascinated, watching the scene.

If only you could have seen the older one watching his brother out of the corner of his eye. He put the bottle to his lips and, pretending to drink, closed his lips tightly so that not a drop got into his mouth.

Then he handed over the bottle, saying to his brother:

'Your turn now. Don't take too much.'

And the young fellow swallowed as much as he could at one gulp.

'Now it's my turn again.' And he repeated the same act as before, completely unaware that I was watching him. He lifted the bottle, now half empty, to his lips, but kept them tightly closed.

'Now your turn.'

'Now my turn.'

'Now me.'

'Now you.'

And in three, four, five, six gulps the little fellow with the curly hair, round tummy and half a shirt finished the bottle of milk.

Tears came to my eyes as I listened to that gypsy child saying to his brother: 'Your turn, my turn.'

With the gypsies' laughter in the background, I began to make my way up the Alhacaba hill, crowded with gypsy children. Half way up, I turned to look back. I felt like going back and taking the bottle, to keep it as a treasure. But it was out of the question. Between a line of donkeys laden with earthen jugs, about ten youngsters were running after the bottle. It was being kicked about by the black feet, bare, dirty, dusty-grey feet, grey like the dust of the road. The generous child was playing with them as naturally as if he had done nothing extraordinary, rather, as naturally as one who is quite accustomed to doing extraordinary things.

There you have it, parents; that is how we are to love one another. The love Christ preached to us demands that kind of thoughtfulness. If our love of God does not make us bite our lips so that our child, our brother, our friend, can drink all the milk in the bottle, then it is not love of God. What an example those blessed gypsies gave me, who am now sitting here writing about charity.

How good God is, to have inscribed on the hearts of men the very words that Jesus used at the Last Supper: 'Love one another; the mark by which all men will know you for my disciples will be the love you bear one another.'

How good God is, to have written on the hearts of those gypsies the very cry that John uttered from Patmos: 'Love one another in deed and in truth.'

How good God is, to have engraved on the heart of every living man the very words that we read in the Gospel outlining all the things we must do on earth: 'Thou shalt love the Lord thy God with the love of thy whole heart, and thy whole soul, and thy whole mind, and thy whole strength . . . and thou shalt love thy neighbour as thyself.'

If a boy has learned to close his lips to milk so that his young brother may have the whole bottle, do you think there will be any need to tell him that he must not harm or slander or defame or injure his brother?

If you think you can live charity without having genuine human affection, then I want none of that 'charity'; I much prefer the love of the gypsy children. The love, the affection between parents and children, has no time to calculate or measure or even care who has given most.

We must forget ourselves and give ourselves completely to others, like that little gypsy who was only ten years old, who wore an old torn trousers and whose feet were covered with the dirt and dust of the road, but who had a big heart, too big to think of himself and forget others.

3

BRIGHT, CHEERFUL HOMES

LIGHT AND JOY

'Your homes must be bright and cheerful (Bl Josemaría).

Your home will be bright[1] if it directs the lives of your
children properly. A bright home is a piece of earth trans-
planted from heaven, where the children learn those
guiding principles concerning God, life, death, man, the
world and love. The success of parents as educators of
their children is assured, not so much by using the
proper means, as by making sure that the ends are
clearly and definitely set out and understood. And the
children learn little by little without any words being
used, by watching the life of Christ lived by their parents. It is not for nothing that Christ is the Light; and
with him, the home cannot but be cheerful. Where there
is light there can be no depression, because the meaning of life is well understood.

That brightness and happiness flow from the love of
which we have already spoken. There will be no need for
you to go around madly trying to find happiness. It is not
a question of creating an artificial atmosphere around
you: it is not even a question of smiling. You will be happy
and you will smile quite naturally if you live a life of love.

The gypsy child could hardly be sad, holding the empty
bottle. He was happy, not because of what he had – for
he had nothing – nor because of what he had given – a
miserable bottle of milk – but because of what he was.
Happiness is within us. It is a great gift, that cannot be

purchased with all the gold on earth. It is a gift of the Holy Ghost.

'Never did rich harvests of corn and wine bring gladness like the gladness Thou puttest in my heart' (Psalm 4, 8).

The Lord tells us: 'I will see you again, and then your hearts will be glad; and your gladness will be one which nobody can take away from you' (John 16, 22).

Do you realise fully that the man who is with God must necessarily be cheerful? Cheerfulness and good humour are something we carry within us, something that makes us happy, even if we have no material goods whatever. If your home lacks cheerfulness then there is something wrong with the way you are living your Christianity. There is something you have not fully understood. Even the darkest and most difficult days bring, every one of them, their little joys . . . at least for the children of God. Sometimes they bring us an overwhelming joy: at other times, they bring us just sufficient energy to face the difficulties of family life; but always, they bring us the strength and encouragement necessary to overcome dangers, sadness and affliction.

The miracle of the men of God 'consists in knowing how to make heroic verse out of the petty prose of each day' (Blessed Josemaría).

However, it is good to foster cheerfulness, which is a consequence of living our divine filiation properly.

You must root out from your home even the tiniest weeds of sadness. Root them out with all your energy. 'Do you not understand that sadness is the worst of all spirits and the most terrible for the servants of God? There is no spirit which so corrupts man.' And again I quote from the same Pastor of Hermas: 'Remove grief from you and crush not the Holy Spirit which dwells in you . . . Cleanse yourself from this wicked grief, and you will live to God.'

Envy, too, must be put aside with all your energy, for it is the cause of sadness. Then you will be free to devote yourself to the conquest of joy.

Explain to your children that the warning 'Woe to those who laugh' does not refer to healthy cheerful laughter, but to the noisy laughter of the stupid, the malicious, the injurious, and to the laughter that shows an evil mind.

Keep your family cheerful, cheerful and amused. Contribute to their joy and amusement in every way. 'Under the reign of boredom nothing great is desired', Chevrot tells us; and great desires are the first steps on the road to sanctity and to the great undertakings which we have to achieve. During that period when your daughter is becoming a young woman and your son is growing into a man, think up every means you can to keep them from being bored. Boredom comes from idleness, which is the worst enemy of children at that stage of their life.

I must repeat once again: your children must have a home that is full of cheerfulness, amusement and warmth.

'My father', a child told me once, 'is always in good humour, but my mother wallops me for nothing.'

They must see you, both of you, in good humour all the time. They need an atmosphere of peace, of tranquillity, of equilibrium, of serenity; an atmosphere in which there will be difficulties, because these cannot be avoided, but no complications.

There are some tragic parents, unbearable parents, who have never been cheerful and can never infuse cheerfulness into their home. I must warn you, parents, that almost all the bad-tempered, the neurotic, the embittered, are children of gloomy parents.

There are some intolerable parents who regard anything as a good excuse for a scolding. They scold not because the child is bold or careless, but because they are annoyed at their own failure to make this child behave perfectly.

You are irritable, so unchristian in fact. You are impossible to live with. I promise you that if you go on like that you will completely deform your children.

You must bear in mind that the formation of your children's personality depends, to a great extent, on how you solve the ordinary little unexpected and innumerable problems that crop up in your everyday family life. Knocking over a glass of water is no reason to send the child to eat in the kitchen. But you are so intolerant! And then you want the child to control himself and stop crying. What can you expect? Who is supposed to give him an example of self-control? 'Do not rouse your children to resentment' (Ephesians 4, 4).

Try to foster a spirit of cheerfulness. Celebrate the great feastdays of the Church and of the family as good children of God. This should be done even if you have to go without soup for the whole of the preceding week to do so. Not that there is any need to spend a fortune on these celebrations; for children all that is necessary is to put out the best table cloth and serve the favourite dish. And they should realise, from an early age, that on your birthday they should have the pleasure of doing something for you. Here again we find cheerfulness and the spirit of service closely bound up with one another.

Don't deprive your little girl of five or six of the experience of helping to get the breakfast ready. Let them all begin to help, boys and girls, as soon as they are able, in the big and little tasks of the home.

A good mother once asked me: 'For me it is quite easy to love my children; will God reward me for this quite spontaneous love I have for them?' How can you doubt it for a moment? Do you think the Blessed Virgin had to make a big effort to embrace her Child? It would be disgraceful if a Christian mother had to offer to God the mortification of being with her children!

You tell me that you find it natural to have a loving affection for your husband? Of course, why not? Do you think that Mary and Joseph did not love one another in a holy manner? God ordains things in this way, and God does everything well. You seem to think there is merit only in what is difficult. With that odd way of thinking you might imagine, in your complicated way, that it would have been better for the disciples to feel sad even when they had the joy of being with Christ after his resurrection! There is no need to get things upside down like this.

What makes you think that heaven can be purchased only at the cost of sorrow on earth? Indeed, how can we be sad, even if there is pain and sorrow, when we know that in heaven we have a God who loves us infinitely?

Love, be happy and be cheerful when the Lord sends you love, happiness and cheerfulness. And love, be happy and be cheerful in the same way when he asks you to do things which you dislike.

Everything should have a positive orientation in your home. It should not be your aim, for instance, to 'put up with' one another, or to 'tolerate' one another. You will find no joy in that attitude. Let your aim be to begin again along the way of love, since marriage is precisely the way of sanctity along the path of human love.

HUMAN VALUES IN THE HOME

I have told you how our homes must be very much alive, and how Christ is to be the central character there, obeyed by parents and children alike. But if we do not live faith, hope and charity in our homes, how can they be called Christian?

Now I want to obviate some possible misinterpretations of this.

The home – and make sure you get this clear – must always be a home; and no excess of enthusiasm on the part of some parents should try to convert it into a monastery.

Those people are very much mistaken who want to destroy all the values of this world. For instance, Christians will never try, can never try – and if anyone does, he is completely wrong – to replace classical or modern music in the home by spiritual hymns. It would be equally wrong to replace all picture magazines by mission news, or family photographs by holy pictures (or wine by holy water . . .). A Christian house should never give the impression of being a religious art exhibition.

However Christian you want to be, you must not try to substitute reading a spiritual book for reading the newspaper. Read your newspaper every day and also do your period of spiritual reading, which you certainly need.

'There is no question whatever', says Canon Thils, 'of substituting a religious community for the family, or pious exercises for study.'

A mother who wants to be Christian must not ignore the current fashions. 'Fashions should be followed in so far as they are intelligent and practicable; they should be avoided and cast aside in so far as they are capricious, voluble, extravagant, mistaken. Help your children to find elegance, good taste and "genuine" fashion in simplicity.'

And this mother, Maria Luisa Guarnero, knows a lot about education; she continues: 'We mothers should teach our daughters, above all by our example, to find the hair style, the cut of their dresses and the colour of cloth which suit their figure best, avoiding carelessness or bad taste.'

I may add that a mother has a duty to be careful about her own appearance, to be elegant, attractive and pleasing to her husband, just as she had a right to be careful about those same things before they were married.

Do you think – as some seem to – that you are a better Christian because you are hideously dressed?

And if for some reason you do not want your daughter to follow the fashion, at least get them to clean their shoes. I am not saying this just to say something, because I know of at least one boarding school, though not for girls, where it is considered 'vanity' to clean one's shoes. Please: we are coming to the end of the twentieth century! Is it then also vanity to clean one's teeth?

'He is a first-class doctor', I was told of a certain man; 'he never goes to the movies except to see the odd religious film.' I am afraid I understood little of that nonsense, but I think it is clear that the 'first class doctor' had no idea whatever of how a man of the world should behave.

The Christian home must remain a home, just as a man who is holy must remain a man. If he, in order to be holy, cannot cease to be a man, in the same way a home, in order to be Christian, must preserve in every way its genuinely human character and its own particular nature. To christianise the homes of the world is to breathe life into those purely human realities; to inspire, direct, transfigure the homes internally, but without destroying their own character. Everything normal and human must remain genuinely 'normal' and 'human'. The only thing that Christ and his Church ask of us is that everything be perfected and ordered by grace. All the things of this world, including the home, should be impregnated and 'informed' by the spirit of Christ lived by those who dwell there. But this impregnating or 'informing' what is profane must never mean transforming it into something religious or monastic. It is different, and I agree that you should complain, when you see little boys dressed for their First Communion in completely unnatural clothes. It is just as bad to dress them as sailors for their First Communion as to dress them as bishops for a procession.

If you like music you will agree with me that it is very pleasant to hear a grand piano well played; and we will also agree that the sound of a good guitar is beautiful. But . . . it would be horrible to have a piano that produced a sound like a guitar.

When you have a children's party in your house, make sure the boys do not dress up as little girls. And make sure that that is not done in the schools either. Of course boys like to dress up, but they should not be allowed to change their sex or their lay state on any of these occasions. I can never understand why people like to dress up their children as monks. To be a priest or a monk is much too serious for that kind of play-acting.

You will not fulfil your duty of infusing a Christian spirit into the family by trying to imitate the spirit of priests or religious. It is not that their spirit is bad, indeed it is admirable; but it is not appropriate, it is not suitable. Your spirit must be one of lay or secular Christians. Sanctity is essentially one, but when we speak of different 'spiritualities' we refer to the many facets in that process of becoming saints. You have a particular vocation to follow, so concentrate on it.

The Christian family must, therefore, be the same as any other family, that is to say, lay – because the members are lay people, not clerics – but with a new way of life, which is the Christian way of life.

How is it that you cannot get into your head, once and for all, just what Christ wants to achieve with this 'profane' or 'non-religious' world? It almost looks as if you are one of those who think that the world and the home are something bad in themselves! The truth is quite the contrary: they are beautiful and good. God has never said otherwise. You will find in Sacred Scripture that the Lord looked on the fruit of his hands in the six-day creation and he saw, not only that it was all good, but that it was very good: 'et erant valde bona' (Genesis 1, 31).

So the home must be impregnated, filled, with the spirit of laymen and not of clerics, a lay not a religious spirit. And if you want to choose Christian magazines for your home, you must choose them by applying, not the standards of religious publications, but the standards of all the ordinary healthy magazines in the world, imbued, as I have so often said, with a Christian spirit.

You may sometimes have heard such phrases as: 'But surely the Church must influence everything we do?' Certainly it must, but do you think the Church is composed only of priests, religious and nuns? You too make up the Church. 'The laity not only belong to the Church', said Pope Pius XII, 'but they constitute it . . . They are the Church.' It is up to you, in a direct and immediate way, to integrate and establish all things, every earthly reality, in Christ.

A home is Christian if the father, the mother and the children live with Christ; and the more desirous they are of achieving perfection, the more Christian will it be. 'A family is Christian when its love is directed towards Love . . . and in so far as it is a school of perfection' (Garcia Hoz). The excellence of a family, the main standard by which a home may be judged to be 'good', depends on whether it is directed to its final end: which is to glorify Christ and serve all men. That is the destiny laid down for it by providence, 'so that God may be all in all' (cf I Corinthians 15, 28).

You glorify and praise God, as a family, when you are together in Church, united to the sacrifice of Christ, or when you all join together to pray to his Mother, or when you, as the father and head of the family, read out the consecration of your home to the Holy Family and ask its aid.

And you serve your fellow men, genuinely, when you all help one another – father, mother and children – to live your true vocation as children of God. The family benefits you all when it helps you to achieve your ultimate end. But this ultimate end can never supplant the immediate end; it only perfects it and directs it towards a higher and absolute plane. Canon Thils says: 'Keeping Sunday holy does not preclude recreation: but it reminds us that recreation is genuinely "healthy" and "human" only when, far from being opposed to man's ultimate end, it coincides with it perfectly.'

SIMPLICITY

Get rid of everything that is useless!

This is how your home should be: cheerful, simple, clean, tidy, receptive, with a family atmosphere, with reminders of those who went before you and bore your name, with signs to show that the people who live there love one another, with a style and personal stamp characteristic of you yourselves, where everyone does everything possible to make life more pleasant for the others. There should be nothing ugly there, nothing dirty, nothing unpleasant, nothing morbid, or forbidding, or cold, or silent. It should not be like a hotel. Good taste is not incompatible with poverty. Dirt, dust and disorder are signs of misery (not of poverty, for poverty is clean) and of carelessness, physical carelessness at least, and perhaps moral carelessness too.

If your home is a dirty barracks, you cannot expect it to attract or keep the children. You must look after it in such a way that your children will feel they want to be in it; it must have the light, the warmth, the feeling of peace and well-being which are essential, if everyone is to be comfortable.

And your house must also be . . . open. Open to receive the friends of the parents, and open to receive the friends of the children. 'Those dwelling places which are too tightly closed up, cloistered and almost inaccessible, in which the light and heat from outside do not converge and which do not radiate outwards, like prisons or the deserts of hermits, are not true homes' (Pius XII).

Your home must also be simple, with no extravagance or ostentation.

The mother of the family, always attracted by the element of beauty, will be able to arrange the little things in the home with great affection and attention. And it is her job to be very careful about those details. Her imagination can work wonders with a few pieces of old cloth. But everything must be clean, tidy, with good taste and dignity.

What is of no importance whatever is whether your house is big or small, wide or narrow, high or low, rich or poor. What matters is the spirit you live inside. And this Christian family atmosphere can be found equally in rich homes or in little houses made of mud that almost merge into the poor land around them in the country; because cheerfulness, simplicity, order, mementos, family atmosphere and mutual affection – none of these things can be purchased with money, but only with the spirit of Christ.

It is of no importance whether your home is like that home at Bethany – for Lazarus, Martha and Mary were rich – or like the home at Nazareth – for Joseph and Mary were poor. Jesus was happy in Peter's house, when he cured his mother-in-law; and that was a poor house. He was just as happy in the house of Jairus, when he gave the dead daughter back her life; and that home was rich.

I have met many poor people who will go straight to the Kingdom of heaven because of the way they live their poverty; and I also know many rich people who will surely enter through the gates of that same Kingdom because they live detached from their riches, with a spirit of poverty.

But I also know both poor people and rich who, if they continue as they are, will never enter into that Kingdom, because they live – if only you could see them! – passionately attached to their filthy money, or to their filthy rags, as the case may be.

What I would like – of course there are so many things one would like – is that we should all learn, like Paul, to live in need and in abundance. I would like if we all lived spiritually apart, detached, free from all those things that time turns into mud and dust. Keep your heart detached from all things. Fix it on nothing but God himself. For it is made to love great things. You cannot allow yourself to love money, or comfort, or power, or flesh, or your stomach – and indeed there are many people for whom their stomach has become their god.

Look, parents, you are adoring golden calves, gods made of gold and silver. You are worshipping gods made with your own hands. Such is your spirit of riches! And it is a false spirit! That is the calf that will keep you from getting to heaven.

Your children will learn, through contact with you, to judge, to calculate, to think, and feel as you judge, calculate, think and feel. If your home is not simple, if you are always trying to impress the neighbours, in that unhealthy and evil atmosphere your children will learn to attach prime importance to money, fortune, comfort, influence, and they will end up by being convinced that in this world, whatever one may say, the most important things are pleasure, fortune and the esteem of others.

If you pass on that vile spirit of riches to your children, then you must take the consequences. 'Do not err, my brethren. Those that corrupt families shall not inherit the kingdom of God,' says Saint Ignatius of Antioch.

[1] Sp: *luminoso.*

4

SCHOOLS

COMPLEMENTARY TO THE HOME

Now you have all you need to fulfil God's will: you have children and you have a home; you constitute a Christian family. 'Preserve it and defend it . . . Where anything has been lost . . . build it up again. You can give your children and your young people nothing more precious than the life and perfection of the family' (Pius XII).

I want to speak to you now, although only in passing, about the school because of course the family cannot do everything. The work done in the home will have to be supplemented by what is done at the school, of whatever type it may be.

But remember, first of all, that the formation given at school is only supplementary. You cannot take the fact that your children go to school as an excuse for neglecting their training at home. At best the education given in a school is, as Pope Pius XII said, 'necessarily imperfect'. It is you, the parents, who are always the principal educators; you must always bear this in mind. It will always be you who are primarily and principally responsible for the way your children are formed.

Nevertheless the school and the teachers do have a share in the tremendous responsibility of educating Christian men.

REFORMATORIES

Here are words of Pius XII: 'Boarding-school education has given good results in the past and is still doing so. Recently, however, it has been the object of severe criticism on the part of certain experts in education. They would like to see it abolished as though it were totally inept. But their criticisms . . . do not constitute a sufficiently good reason for a sweeping condemnation of this type of education in itself.'

What we must all try to do – it is only right that we should – is to have 'school-homes', that is to say, schools which would be a continuation of the home, schools which, simply because they are such would not have to give the impression of being barracks, or prisons, or reformatories, or business institutions.

Why should our boys and girls have to spend years and years in reformatories before being let live their lives normally? What have they done to be made study behind barred windows, surrounded by dust and dirty furniture? A school-home keeps everything clean. Any school or college, however poor, can always be clean, very clean, like a good home. We can have schools that are very poor and very clean. But we can also build great and magnificent buildings that look like prisons inside and outside.

I can assure all you teachers that it is quite possible to keep the children's desks clean, if you want to do so. It all depends on how determined you are and on how much importance you attach to cleanliness. If you cannot get the children to feel that the things in the school are theirs, then it will never be like a home. And how can they be expected to feel that the things in the school are theirs when everywhere there is an air of carelessness and dirt? In every home, however simple or humble, when a bulb fuses or a window pane breaks, it is replaced. Then you must see to it that the same is done at school. Neglect or carelessness must never be regarded as a virtue.

It is true that I have begun this subject on a material level but you cannot shirk your responsibility by saying that these things are of no importance, because they are. They show lack of order, of propriety, of good taste. How can such a school ever be a continuation of the home?

Teachers, be sure you foster the human virtues in your pupils. Teach them to rectify those virtues and raise them up, with the help of the divine grace, to a supernatural level. For instance, are you sure you attach sufficient importance to the question of order? And yet, without order, there can be no virtue.

Perhaps some years ago you started out with great ideals. Well, why have you allowed yourself to grow old and disillusioned? You know you must keep renewing yourself all the time. And yet you have let that cursed routine spirit to take hold on you and it has crept into all the methods and systems you use. And acting through mere routine or out of habit will destroy any centre of education, however good it may be; in fact, it spoils everything men try to do.

The fact that parents expect a good report means nothing, because, in general, parents know very little about pedagogy. For them the great triumph – among other things – they like to tell their relatives and friends about so proudly, is that their son of such an age has passed a very difficult examination. But you must not pander to these vanities. Proud parents, I must ask you one thing: have you ever thought of asking the teachers whether that triumph was really merited? What interests me, and what should interest you, is to know the mental age of the child, and then you will be in a position to decide whether to regard his success as genuine or whether, although he has passed the examination, he would be well advised to repeat the year.

Remember, teachers, you have sometimes to educate both the children and the parents.

We teachers must all try to be younger than our years. We have to be young in spirit, full of enthusiasm and delight in being with the children. There is no use whatever in our 'mortifying' ourselves by living among them. The child wants to see in his teacher a friend, not a monster or prison warder.

Certainly it is very easy to growl and scowl all the time, so that they do not misbehave in the classroom. It is much more difficult to be their friend in class and outside, but this is far more effective.

It is much simpler to mete out in each case the punishment laid down by the rules for each offence, than to punish them in a personal way, without losing your temper, using arguments based on reason and affection . . . But this is a better method, because it is more like what happens in a home than what happens in a prison. '... Discipline ... so rigid as not to distinguish one individual from another undoubtedly has its dangers', says Pope Pius XII. 'Even small errors in method can produce boys who will have anything but a sense of personal responsibility. Because of their mechanical discharge of their duties, their study, discipline and prayer unconsciously become mere matters of form. Strict uniformity tends to suffocate personal initiative; a secluded life to restrict a wide vision of the world. An inflexible insistence on rules sometimes gives rise to hypocrisy, or imposes a spiritual level which for one will be too low and for another, on the contrary, unattainable. Excessive severity ends by making rebels of strong characters, while the timid become depressed and secretive.'

I understand – of course I understand – how you feel when you say you have had enough of children. But when a teacher begins to get a headache from the noise the children make during the break, the best thing he can do is take some pills for the headache and then get a different kind of job. If the noise of children upsets you, instead of getting them to be quiet it is you who should be quiet . . . and go somewhere else.

It is nothing but that same routine spirit that allows a teacher to relax during the breaks, forgetting that he should be at least as active then as when he is explaining a difficult point in class. It is that routine spirit that allows a teacher to give a class without preparing it, because he thinks he knows it already. Perhaps he does, but what he does not know is that an unprepared lesson is of very little value. Never think that to give a class is to repeat what the children can read for themselves in the book!

What steps do you take to awaken the interest of the pupils at the beginning of your class? Those classes in which only the teacher speaks should be left for the university. In your lessons the pupils must take an active part; the class must be full of life. They must fully understand the points they are going to study alone, later in the day.

When I was young I often wondered why they had gone to the trouble of buying all that equipment for physics, which was only left there in glass cases covered with dust. Undoubtedly at some time someone full of enthusiasm had put them there, but then with time his enthusiasm had become covered with dust because he too had got into a rut.

And if you have got into bad habits and prefer to go on with those out-of-date methods of discipline, then that is your affair. Personally I prefer a school-home and many parents agree with me – where the child is happy, full of confidence and in an atmosphere of friendship.

When are we going to get rid of detention as a method of punishment? We still detain the children in the schools, forgetting that this is a survival from the days of Napoleon. We never seem to notice that it is always the same offenders who are detained week after week. We refuse to see that this method is useless. It is always the same pupils who are deprived of their 'free days' and it also seems to be the same teachers who impose that punishment. Surely the time has come to try new methods.

And there are many other examples of this routine spirit. There are, for instance, those collective punishments that we have all suffered. This is the nearest thing imaginable to mass executions. It is always an injustice, an injustice used as a means of defence by the mediocre teacher.

'It is one of the laws of life that children are never quite alike, either in intelligence or in character or in other spiritual qualities. When, therefore, one is arranging their way of life, or correcting or judging them, this individuality must be borne in mind' (Pius XII). 'Both supervision and punishment must be personal, doubly personal. They should come from a person and not from a system: they should be explained in a certain tone of voice and with a definite intention, and not simply written in a register; they should also be aimed at a definite person and not at an anonymous or "standard" pupil. They should be directed towards the tendencies and tastes of the child, and not calculated merely arithmetically according to "hours of detention" and "days of punishment"' (Le Gall).

Any teacher who has to punish or threaten to punish the pupils in order to keep silence in his class shows that he is not really convinced of what he is teaching, that he has no interest in teaching it, and has no understanding of the mentality of his pupils. Perhaps he may make a wonderful lecturer for more mature people, but he is not a good teacher.

A pompous teacher who refuses to admit his mistakes and insists that 'The teacher is always right', as well as telling lies (because a teacher makes mistakes like everyone else) is unwise and will never form his pupils properly.

So let us have no collective punishments and no unreasonable personal punishments.

It may seem strange, but there are still teachers who try to correct their pupils by making them write out five hundred times the line 'Procrastination is the thief of time'. Do you think the poor child knows what 'procrastination' is? Perhaps you are not too clear yourselves. And even if you are, you can take it from me that the only thing achieved by that method is that they will spoil their handwriting by scribbling 'procrastination' as fast as they can five hundred times. Can we not think up other more helpful punishments?

Every impersonal, excessive or harsh punishment creates a bad atmosphere in the school. And if to those unwise methods of keeping discipline, you add a system involving rows of pupils, almost complete anonymity, treatment of each pupil as just a number among thousands of others, lack of personal concern for them, frequent public humiliation, then you will have a prison atmosphere that will drive the pupils frequently to deceit, lies and insincerity as means of protection against pain and humiliation.

MONASTERIES

Having said that a school is not meant to be a kind of prison reformatory, we must also say that neither is it meant to be a monastery or convent.

It seems to be a fairly widespread custom in schools to saturate the children with pious acts, with far more of them than you would expect to find in any Christian home. Compulsory daily Mass, long prayers, many sermons, frequent Solemn Benedictions and so on. 'This is done with the idea – indeed a very true idea in the abstract – that piety is useful in everything and so the more of it the better. If we inquire whether the pupils are expected to keep up all these practices throughout their future life, we will be told that probably they will not, but that at least it is good for them to do a lot of them for several years while they are young and in that way they acquire regular habits, and that if they drop some of the practices later on, they will be more likely to keep some of them than if their acts of devotion had been less while they were at school. To this we answer', says Fr Hull, 'that it is all very well when that system gives good results; in some cases it will work out well. But in the majority of cases it is more likely not to work out at all; and in those cases where it does fail, the failure will be absolutely disastrous.'

On such a delicate subject as this, the best thing to do is to listen to the authoritative words of Pope Pius XII: 'There have been cases of pupils of schools, even Catholic schools, where moderation has been disregarded, where an effort has been made to impose a tenor of religious practices which would be disproportionate perhaps even for seminarists, so that these pupils, when they return home to their families, neglect even the most elementary duties of a Christian, such as attendance at Sunday Mass. Certainly young people must be helped and exhorted to pray; but always in a measure such that the prayer will be a sweet necessity of the soul.'

And the same Pope said: 'Even pious exercises must be in a proper measure, so that they do not become an almost unbearable burden and provoke weariness in the soul.'

BUSINESS

The idea of 'mass education' or education 'in bulk' will be acceptable only to people who think that education can be treated as a business. I once saw an example of this, where the headmaster and parent in question were both equally amazed at the other's attitude.

'You cannot really expect me to know your three sons, when we have hundreds and hundreds of boys in the school.'

But the parent's reply was overwhelming:

'Why shouldn't you know them?' he said angrily: 'They're triplets!'

A very bad principal of a school once said to me: 'When the parents of some pupil ask me about their son, I always answer the same thing: that he should study harder. How can I be expected to know them all?' But you are wrong, my friend.

I know that the present circumstances put teachers in a position where they have to deal with thousands of pupils. Well, if that is the case it is not their fault, but it means that we shall go on with 'mass production' education. In this way we can teach the dates of the chief battles, the rivers of Asia and Africa and a few other facts, but we cannot educate, we cannot form, anybody.

'Instruction acts only on the intellect; education is concerned with the will, the sentiments, the morals, the taste, the highest aspirations of the child; it loses sight neither of his individual nor of his social being; its purpose is the harmonious development of all the potentialities which God has placed in the child' (Kieffer).

THE SCHOOL-HOME

A school-home is, by definition, the very opposite of a school run merely as a business.

'It is essential that each one should feel himself to be the object of special attention on the part of the educator and should never get the impression of being confused or forgotten in the mass, neglected as to his particular needs, demands or weaknesses, as if only his physical presence counted' (Pius XII).

Any school or college will form its pupils well, or not so well, according as it resembles a Christian home, that is to say, a place where the child is not treated as a number, but is taken seriously and known by his name, a person whose mental age is known, whose virtues, likes and dislikes, manner of studying, tastes and character are recognised, whose capabilities and difficulties as regards study are appreciated and, of course, whose parents and home atmosphere are known and taken into account.

We need school-homes where intelligence and aptitude tests are used, not to find out the traits and inclinations of the pupils, but only to corroborate what the teachers already know of them.

'Such care for each one of the pupils will arouse in them a sufficient stimulus to affirm and develop their personal temperament, their spirit of initiative, their sense of responsibility towards their superiors and colleagues in the same way as they would in the bosom of a numerous and well ordered family' (Pius XII).

In a school-home, as in a good family, personal and collective responsibility should be fostered, the one being as important as the other. Our children must be taught to work as part of a team.

It is good to encourage pupils to strive for personal improvement; a healthy pride is very effective in every way. But let us have no competitive rivalry. I refer to that rivalry which consists of praising some while hurting others, and this is not Christian. We must avoid all signs of one-upmanship in our classes.

'The atmosphere in some classes, continually disrupted by classifications and changing places, putting the victors up to the top and the vanquished down to the bottom, is deplorable. We have even seen – in a class which in other respects was excellent – a "dishonours list". This aggressive type of rivalry, which allows one to reach the top but only over the dead body of another, is a heresy for them all.

'An intelligent teacher can let each pupil know the faults and the progress he is making without having to compare them with the faults and progress of others. What need is there to award marks for the compositions?' (Le Gall).

All this requires a great effort, we cannot deny that; but teachers are there surely for something more than just to talk about subjects. And all the teaching staff in a school should be as much in agreement on the objects and aims to be achieved with the pupils, as should the parents be in the home.

I know many very good schools, and in all of them I have found one great virtue floating in the atmosphere: great ambition and enthusiasm for the formation and training of the pupils. And this spirit avoids all sense of routine. If you want to instil that home atmosphere into your school – and I assure you that you can do so if you want to – then first of all you must live it yourselves. It will all depend on the objects you have set yourselves to attain. It will depend on those few ideas you have set up for the education of the children.

The impossible will then become possible, and not only possible but true. For instance, among other things, the punishment of not being allowed to come to school will become a reality! But also something much more important: an atmosphere of sincerity and loyalty will be built up where there will be immense mutual respect and great friendship and confidence between pupils and teachers.

Once this atmosphere and spirit of a Christian home is achieved, there will be no more need for lining up the pupils, collective punishments, classifications, clouting or honours lists.

5

GOD'S COMMANDS

POPULATE THE EARTH

> *You must make the effort to fulfil generously the duty of fecundity (Pius XII).*

I have spoken at some length about the environment in which your children should be brought up, if they are to develop as men and as Christians. I have tried to show that rearing a family is a tremendous responsibility but at the same time a rewarding one when it is done with love of God and with a firm conviction that your own search for the perfection God asks of you lies mainly in the generous fulfilment of your family duties.

However, there is one cardinal family duty which has today become the subject of confused thinking: I refer to the very *having* of children. Allow me to speak strongly about this, while there is still time.

So you have children? How many?

Don't forget that God has the power to raise up children out of the very stones on the ground. And in spite of that, he still wants you to collaborate with him in this matter. Be careful not to distort or misinterpret the vocation he has given you: God himself is asking you for children. Twenty centuries ago he cursed a fig-tree just because it was not producing fruit.

'Foolish indeed, ignorant of themselves and unhappy are those mothers who complain when a new child clings to them and asks to be fed at the fountain of their breasts' (Pius XII).

It is God himself who asks you to sanctify your married life by fulfilling that very first end of marriage. You must have children; you must yield fruit. If you do not have children, you will end up by having dogs instead!

A good mother I knew used to say to me: 'Nowadays very few people speak of the duty to have children.' Yes, indeed, very few people speak about that duty. So, do try to realise that we must tell everyone and make them understand what God demands of them.

In many bookshops I have found an enormous number of books and pamphlets discussing the various methods of not having children without actually committing sin. Pages and pages deal with this same subject. We always seem to want to go as far as possible while just keeping outside the strict definition of sin. And I find no attempt to encourage us to raise our eyes on high – nothing like the great generosity with which our Father God treats us. We men are certainly very mean.

The self-centeredness that we find nowadays, and which is the cause of all the crises we are going through, has incited many people to make a detailed and precise study of the sterile and fertile periods, with the one purpose of making calculations, pandering to their meanness, their selfishness, their determination to have all the pleasure they can without any responsibility and without having children.

You can take it from me: the only one who gets any good or any benefit out of all this selfishness is the devil; he is more interested than anyone else in having the fewest possible number of children in heaven. And those people are playing right into his hands; they are playing a dirty game, and the pity is that sometimes – often – they do it out of a misdirected sense of consideration for the upbringing of the couple of children they already have.

If those people were pagans, I would not mind so much hearing them speak all the time of birth prevention. What else could we expect? But they are Catholics, so we cannot let it go on.

What a convenient loss of memory! Have they forgotten that it was God who told us: 'Increase and multiply' and again 'Populate the earth'? To increase, multiply and populate the earth with Christians is a blessing and at the same time a command from God to those who, by divine vocation, have been called to produce men, 'so that through you the multitude of God's children may increase and the number of the elect be completed' (Pius XII).

Parents, have you forgotten what your dignity requires of you? Have you forgotten that you are collaborators with God in the act of transmitting life? You call the body into being and God completes your work by creating a new and distinct soul for each child. You are, as it were, participants of that power with which God first created man from clay.

God asks you to have children because he 'needs' them. He has a right to demand the birth of new men into your family. From among them he will then choose heroes, hard workers, priests, spreaders of his Gospel, people to live in the world or apart from the world, completely consecrated to his service. From among them he will choose soldiers and unconquerable leaders; he will choose future fathers and mothers who will enjoy no rest perhaps on this earth but will enjoy in the next world all the glory achieved by their children. From among them he will choose 'the successors of his first Vicar in the universal government of his flock' (Pius XII).

'The inheritance of the Lord are children: the reward, the fruit of the womb' (Psalm 126). 'Did not he make them one? . . . And wherefore one? That they might seek a godly seed' (Malachias 2, 15). 'Woman will find her salvation in child-bearing', Saint Paul reminds us.

'Were you not therefore freely united in the sacrament . . . before God . . . to ask him, freely and devoutly, for these souls which he is eager to entrust to you?' (Pius XII).

Parents, I am now speaking to you in a very low voice, and I assure you that if the love of a husband and wife does not end in the birth of children, then they have murdered that love. The love of man and wife demands children, for genuine love, true love, tends towards them as its natural end.

MEAN SOULS

Parents, do you want to give your children good teachers? Then give them many brothers and sisters!

I know you are now looking around for some means to justify yourself. I know too that you see other families without children. I know children are almost disappearing, both in cities and in the country, from rich homes and poor homes, from high up and low down. Yes, I know that if you suggest having many children people will look at you as if you were mad. 'Nowadays?' they say. 'In this modern age? With all the present-day difficulties? You are quite mad.' And to confuse you all the more, they will come along with quotations from bad books; they will swamp you with reasons, political, social and economic. 'The population of the world is increasing at an alarming rate . . . A day will come when the earth will no longer be able to produce food for all its inhabitants.'

Tell them that that is not true! Tell them that the soil of the earth will always give its fruit if men do their work as God commands. In many cases it is the soil of their souls that is bad and yields no fruit. Tell them that those present-day difficulties, such as the high cost of living and low incomes, are often mere lies glossed over with a little truth and passed off as excuses to avoid doing the will of God.

I know the present-day problems intimately. And I know there are many persuasive reasons why this or that particular family might not wish to have more than, say, three children. But you will never convince me with your petty arguments that that is the correct solution to their problems. The rich seem to have less children than the poor. The statistics are very enlightening: the lowest birth rates are to be found in some of the richest areas.

Let me tell you the only reason why you do not want to have children, so that you can think about it and see if it is a justification for your barrenness: it is the lack of a Christian spirit in your family. There is no other reason, believe me. You have decided not to realise – it would be so inconvenient – that to be a disciple of Christ always involves taking up your cross and following a path that leads to sacrifice. In order to rise again we must die first: you have decided to forget that. And if you will not listen to me, I will only go on reminding you: To be a Christian means self-sacrifice and heroism. Sanctity means living all that our Christian vocation involves, down to the last detail.

I would like to have seen you nineteen hundred years ago when to be a Christian carried the death penalty. I am certain that many of those same people who nowadays refuse to have children would have continued offering incense to the idols, as much incense as necessary because any amount of it would have been cheaper than losing their life.

What they want is to have all the pleasures of married life while avoiding the duties that go with them. But they will never admit this; instead, they try to cover up their selfishness with the outward signs of Christianity. They are turning the dignity of matrimony, blessed by

Christ himself, into a poor, cheap, vulgar commerce in human flesh. They are like the sellers in the temple. They are miserly, mean, cowardly, selfish, comfort-loving, avaricious, lustful, lazy. Let us add up these qualities and see what we get. At school we learned to add like this:

> Miserliness
> Meanness
> Cowardice
> Selfishness
> Love of comfort
> Avarice
> Lust
> Laziness
> ─────────────
> Total: Birth prevention

Whatever you do, never be guilty of deliberately destroying life. Birth prevention is an insult to providence and to the cross that Christ carried.

You remind me, and quite rightly, that our holy Mother the Church has spoken on this subject and has allowed some exceptional cases. Of course there are exceptional cases! But you seem to have made them into a general rule. Everything must be taken in its proper context.

There are cases where it is quite legitimate to limit the number of children one will have. I am speaking now to Christians and I must remind you that in no case can this ever be done by means which are intrinsically wrong in themselves, means which militate against the law of God or go against the marital act. No circumstances, however grave or exceptional, can justify such means.

It is legitimate to limit the number of one's children by making use of the periods of natural sterility, the 'safe' periods, when there are grave reasons – and not otherwise – of a medical, eugenic, economic or social nature. But it must be made quite clear that love of comfort, selfishness, sensuality, avarice or laziness can never be grave reasons.

'But if such grave reasons, either personal or resulting from external circumstances, are absent', says Pius XII, 'then the intention habitually to avoid the fruitfulness of the union, while it continues to give full satisfaction to sensuality, can only derive from a false outlook on life and from motives foreign to the correct ethical norms.'

I suppose you would like me now to set out these grave reasons that may justify limiting the number of children, going into all the details. But I am not going to do that. If you think your case constitutes an exception, then go and consult the proper person. But before you look for advice, let me tell you this: There are many sick people who are insincere, and they go from one doctor to another until at last they find one who will allow them to smoke and drink. I am sure you see what I mean. There are many ways of presenting your case.

There is, however, one wonderful method of limiting births, which is quite compatible with the greatest desires of perfection. This method is, of course, continence (cf I Cor 7, 5).

But for all those who try to take refuge hypocritically behind the Church's doctrine in order to continue playing their games, let me quote here the words of Pope Pius XII. If you want to know the best conduct for a Christian, the truly sanctifying conduct, then here are the Pope's words: 'Our special congratulations and our paternal gratitude go to those generous married couples who, for love of God and trusting in him, courageously bring up a numerous family . . . The individual and society, the nation and the state, even the Church itself, depend for their existence, according to the order established by God, on fruitful marriages.' I am not go-

ing to repeat these words to you, but I want you to read
them again.

And the Pope continues: 'Therefore to embrace the
married state, to use continually that faculty which is
proper to it and which only within it is legitimate while,
at the same time, deliberately avoiding the primary duty
of that state without grave motive, is to sin against the
very meaning of conjugal life.'

Generosity and confidence in God: these are the two
great reasons for having a large family. And they are
precisely the two virtues I think you lack. Do not ask me
how many children you should have. We are told by a
modern author that 'genuine conjugal love aspires to
the glory of fertility and takes pride in it. But the glory of
fertility cannot be found in fertility measured drop by
drop. It must be an abundant fertility which seeks abundance and has to be given reasons, not for having children, but for limiting their number in any way.'

Neither Christ nor his Church nor any human law
fixes the number of children you should have. I can,
however, tell you that three is the minimum number
necessary if man is not to disappear entirely from the
earth. The other number, the maximum, will be decided
by your own faith, your hope, your love of God, and God's
will.

Parents who do not produce children to occupy the
places reserved for them in heaven are just as guilty as
a priest would be if he did not try to bring Christ to
souls or a Christian who made no effort to spread the
kingdom of Christ in society. The most effective
apostolate that Christian parents can do, the best way
they can win new apostles for Christ, is to have children, many children. Writers sow the seed of written
words, preachers sow the spoken word, theologians sow
doctrine – all working to increase the number of Christ's
followers. But you, parents, sow life itself.

REASONS FOR NOT HAVING CHILDREN

Do not despise that great treasure the Lord is willing to place in your hands. Blessed are those fathers and mothers who have many children, for they are the gifts that God bestows on Christian families.

'Your joy will increase and multiply each time you see Baptism regenerate other little ones', said Pope Pius XII. 'Children's children are the crown of old men: and the glory of children are their fathers' (Proverbs 16, 6). And there is a German saying which tells us that 'many children are many *Paternosters,* many blessings from God, many joys.'

The King of kings, the Almighty, asks you to fulfil perfectly the vocation to which you have been called; he asks you to be fertile, to yield fruit. Parents who have few children and do not want to have any more seek in those they have a certain satisfaction, the satisfaction of perpetuating themselves. These are children of, and for, their selfishness. Parents of large families, on the other hand, always find it easier to understand that their children are not for them but for God. 'A cradle consecrates the mother of a family; many cradles sanctify and glorify her in the eyes of her husband, of her children, of the Church and of the State' (Pius XII).

If the grain of wheat, when it is sown in the ground, does not die, then it remains nothing but a grain of wheat, barren. When we think of this we can hardly be surprised that there is so much barrenness in the world. Many parents want only to live – no question of dying! – and to live as comfortably as possible. They have forgotten these words of Christ about the grain of wheat. They are not willing to die, to make sacrifices. So there will be no fruit, because to have fruit there has to be death and winter, rain and sun, cold and heat. You cannot be surprised, then, to see that the grains of wheat remain sterile. Life cannot be transmitted without sacrifice on the part of the living.

Christians, it seems clear that you are being infected by all the vices and crimes of those others who neither believe nor hope in God. 'They were mingled among the heathens, and learned their works, and served their idols . . . And they sacrificed their sons and their daughters to devils. And they shed innocent blood, the blood of their sons and their daughters which they sacrificed to the idols of Chanaan. And the land was polluted with blood' (Psalm 105).

When you say 'That couple has no children, nor that other . . .' you are looking at pagans. I could also show you many more who are and wish to remain childless. But if the first Christians, instead of living their faith and hope in Christ and in what the newly-born Church demanded of them, had looked around them at what the pagans of their time were doing, they would have continued to do as they did and would have worshipped the gods of stone.

If we go on like that, taking example from everybody around us without discriminating, our churches will soon be filled with a new type of 'Christians-without-cross'; we will have lots of Christians without crosses, who will end up by being surprised to see Christ still hanging painfully from one.

There is a story of a so-called good woman who went into a shop and said: 'I want a crucifix. But it must be a small one, because it is for the bedroom and I don't want it to frighten me.'

We are bearing on our shoulders the dead weight of an age that worships self and tries to avoid all responsibility, and this is often painfully obvious even in the kind of education and training we give young people who are in our charge.

I have often thought that a book could be written entitled *The Minimum Requirements for Entering Heaven.* The publisher of such a book would certainly make a fortune. It would give of course, some ideas on the least number of children one could have while still continuing to be a Christian. A chapter could be devoted to the minimum percentage of our surplus money which we should give the Church in order to fulfil our duty of giving alms. Another chapter could calculate the minimum number of days which must be devoted to our children in order to fulfil the obligation of educating them. Another section, and by no means the least important, could deal with the minimum concern we have to show for our neighbour which would be compatible with that first of God's commandments. A study could also be made of the limits to which a Christian's irresponsibility and abstentionism in public affairs can go before being condemned outright by the Church. But enough of this joking.

If you continue in your present attitude – fruitless, selfish, sterile, useless – you will soon see what kind of children you are bringing up. What will you teach them about God? What can you tell them about Christ? Will you tell them lies, saying that he lived a life of mediocrity, like you?

Anything good that your children may learn outside the home will be completely undone by the example you give them. What will those poor children see in religion?

Now perhaps you will see a meaning behind this hard and bitter thing a child once said to me: 'I would like to be grown up so that I can stop praying, like my father.'

What advice will you give your children? Will you be as stupid as that 'good' mother who advised her son who was in the air-force to 'fly low and slow'?

Go on like that, giving advice that reeks of that sickly thing you call prudence, and I have no idea where you may end up. One thing I can promise you is that you will never see that hundredfold the Lord promised to the generous. The 'hundredfold in this world' is quite incompatible with an attitude that calculates the limits beyond which generosity need not go.

MEN WITHOUT HOPE

Christians nowadays seem to have an erroneous idea that giving implies losing the thing they give. How then can they have a proper understanding of what sanctity involves, when the very first step on the way to sanctity is to forget oneself completely? That is the indispensable condition both for love of God and for love of men.

It is sad that I should have to say this, but believe me, you give the impression of being men with very little faith and very little hope. And that is the root of your lack of generosity. You are willing to do just the bare minimum. You are willing to do what is essential, but only what is absolutely essential, in order to get into heaven – if there is a heaven, that is – but without going too far in anything you do. It would be a pity if, after all, it turned out that there was no God and you had been wasting your time! It is sad that I should have this idea, but it is your own behaviour which makes me write these terrible words.

This is the only explanation of so many things I see you do. This is the only explanation of your pettiness and your 'prudence'. I can see why you pray to God only at night, so that during the day you can concentrate on your own personal pleasures.

You believe sufficiently to go to Church – the gods must not be made angry! – but not sufficiently to work for God. You believe and you hope sufficiently to pray and so keep his wrath turned away from you – punishment does not appeal to you – but you do not believe sufficiently to see that the Lord is taking care of your family. You believe sufficiently to give a few cents to the poor, because you have been taught that the first precept imposed by Christ is the law of charity, but you do not believe sufficiently to give yourself to Christ in your children. You believe sufficiently to ask the priest's blessing when you get married, but not sufficiently to believe that the sacrament of Matrimony continues to help you vigorously and unceasingly throughout your married life. You believe in providence, but not sufficiently to abandon yourself into the hands of the Lord when the question of a large family is to be considered. You believe in God, but not sufficiently to realise that he sees and hears you when you are at work, when you are in your home resting quietly or when you are at play.

What you need is the faith and the hope of a new convert, and then you might emerge from that lukewarm state in which you are wallowing.

6

THE SANCTITY OF PARENTS

FAITH IN CHRIST

> *'Now therefore fear the Lord, and serve him with a perfect and most sincere heart . . . But if it seem evil to you to serve the Lord, you have your choice: choose this day that which pleaseth you, whom you would rather serve, whether the gods which your fathers served in Mesopotamia, or the gods of the Amorrhites, in whose land you dwell. But as for me and my house we will serve the Lord' (Josue 24, 14-15).*

If you are not willing to do what God commands, then rebel against him. You will then at least have taken up a definite attitude towards Christ, because up to now, in spite of what you may pretend, it is clear that you have adopted none.

Christ must be either accepted or rejected. What we cannot do is play games with him or with his commands. But if you decide to accept him, please follow your decision through to its logical conclusions.

One thing quite certain is that when Christ became man he gave his Gospel to all men, to the sixty generations who have gone before us and to those that are to follow. Sooner or later the moment comes when each one of us must ask him that question, as the disciples of John the Baptist did: 'Who are you?' And Christ answered: 'I am the Messias.'

The Jews asked him the same question: 'If you are the Christ, tell us so openly.' But if he answers you, as he answered them, with a clear 'yes', will you also cast stones at him?

Your world and my world – for every soul is a world to itself – must either admit Christ or lock him out, accept him or reject him. He wants no slaves; he wants us to be free, free as the birds of the air, with freedom equalled only by our responsibility. Freely, and responsibly, you can either open or close the Gospel. But what you cannot do is to treat it like any other mere book, to be opened and then thrown down, open at any old page, among piles of other books.

The most important history of all, the deepest and only really transcendental one, the only history that has an absolute value, which reaches to heights of infinite worlds, has never been written, and never will be written because it cannot be: it is your history and the history of each one of your children, your life, made up of dealings and meetings with Christ, of painful meetings, of attitudes adopted by you towards this living Christ.

You say you are not conscious of ever having had such meetings or discoveries, and I admit that you may not have noticed them clearly. But this does not relieve you of your responsibility, because you have too much noise going on in your soul. That is your great downfall: the noise going on in your soul.

Christ knocks again and again, he pleads to be let in and, if you open to him, he enters. But in spite of his knocking and pleading, he remains outside if you close yourself up against him. God does not force souls, for he is good, he loves freedom. And it can happen – unfortunately it does happen – that if you have neither time nor room in your soul nor any desire to receive Christ, then he will remain outside, and you will scarcely see him.

This is the history that will never be written, but which has eternal importance. It is a history made up of many silences, day after day, and it makes up the story of the eighty – eighty or twenty, what matter? – years which you will spend on earth. This is the history which reaches into eternity: the story of your life, made up of your meetings with Christ.

The story of your life, you who are looked down on by others; you who beg for alms, pretending to be pious and resigned to your fate, while at the same time trying to steal everything you can lay your hands on, because your children are hungry. Tell me: do you accept or reject Christ?

And you, poor man who are so rich, with so much money, you who try so hard to avoid meeting the thieving beggar as he stands at the gate of your house, you who have never known what hunger is and want to know nothing about it, tell me: do you freely accept Christ or do you rebel against him? Answer that question, for that is the question on which your life depends.

And you and I, average men, neither very rich nor very poor, have we said 'yes' to Christ, or are we still not quite decided? Life consists of choosing, of opening or shutting the door to the living Christ. Answer, answer him that question.

You see, you have been used to living your faith, your Christianity, out of mere habit. And now all this appears rather strange, because you had never even thought that you had to choose between saying 'yes' and saying 'no' to God.

You are a hard-working man, living a life full of worries, with now and then some amusement; but everything centres around your work, your worries, your amusement. You live in a world into which God, your wife and your children make their way only from time to time. In this stupid way you are wasting your life down here and failing to get a grasp on Life itself. You need a little more faith, a little more hope, a little more love.

Certainly you have faith: you received it at Baptism. But when we take a close look at how lightly you treat your duties as a Christian, we get the impression that the waters of that sacrament only weigh you down heavily.

You have faith in Christ, but you do not live the spirit of that faith. You have a soft heart, you are deeply moved when you hear of physical misfortunes, of cancer cases, of tuberculosis, and you even donate money to relieve the needs which you see with the eyes of your body. But you do not live the spirit of faith: you have no eyes in your soul. You gaze into nothingness when you hear someone speak of God, of the salvation of your children, of the great apostolates which the Church demands of us today.

Have you a sufficient spirit of faith to understand what the Church says concerning children: that they are a gift and a blessing from God?

Have you faith? Perhaps up to now your parents, your brothers and sisters, your family or the environment in which you live have saved you the trouble of making up your mind. But the moment will come – it is called a crisis – when you yourself will have to answer that question. When that moment comes neither your parents, nor your brothers and sisters, nor your family, nor the environment will be of any avail. The answer you give will have to be personal and inalienable. 'Do you believe in the Son of Man?' Christ asked the man born blind. And not his parents but the man himself, for he was of age, had to answer: 'I believe, Lord.'

At the beginning of this book I said I would speak to you about God and your children. Perhaps you hoped I would speak more about them and less about him. But I make no apology for reminding you again that this is the foundation, not only of your own salvation, which is indeed very important, but also of the Christian formation and training of your children.

The specific and immediate purpose of Christian education is to co-operate with divine grace in forming the true and perfect Christian; to express and form Christ himself in those who have been regenerated by Baptism, according to the words of Saint Paul: "My little children, of whom I am in labour again, until Christ be formed in you"' (Pius XI).

I am beginning to think that people do not realise what God expects of them in relation to their children. Look, the one and only thing that matters is this: to help those youngsters to become men, Christians and saints. 'The soundness and efficiency of a school are a matter not so much of good rules as of good teachers', said Pius XI. And the most important teachers that God has given your children are you, their father and their mother.

I can assure you that if you base your life firmly on Christ, all the rest will follow as a direct consequence. If you have faith in Christ, and live with that spirit of faith, your home will be a Christian one; it will have a warm atmosphere where all will be infected with your faith – and what a blessed infection.

If you live by faith, your deeds will radiate hope, even in the pagan climate of these days in which we live.

If you live by faith, your children will learn to treat Christ as an important person in the world today. He will cease to be a mere theory, as he is, unfortunately, for many parents who still have pretensions to Christianity.

If the spirit of faith is lived in your home, your children will learn to pray as God wishes them to pray. If you live by faith, all those problems which weigh so heavily on the parents of today will solve themselves of their own accord. I am sure you have seen, for instance, some parents who rebel against their children's vocation. Well, the root of that rebellion is in their lack of faith.

If you live by faith, there will be no need for me to give you any advice about how to have a good atmosphere in your family. And that atmosphere will do all the rest.

If you live the spirit of faith, truth and freedom will have the honoured place they should have in your home and neither falsehood nor slavery will appear there.

If you live by faith, you will learn to disappear, so that when the moment comes you will be able to let your children go their own way in life.

If you live by faith, by hope and by love, – and if it is God's will – in your home there will be children, many children, and everyone will be loved with the love of children. If you live by faith, you will die, just like those who have no belief, but death for you will give place to life.

All the ways discovered by men end at the same place, the walls of death, and they can go no further. The only way that goes through those walls and leads us on to heaven is called Christ.

SANCTITY IN MARRIAGE

> *'In the eyes of God, all of us, without distinction, are called to sanctity!' (Pope John XXIII)*

Why do you keep on looking at the pharisees? Do you want to be compared with them? You are always looking for an excuse in the negative attitude of those around you in order to continue doing nothing positive.

You are like the barren fig-tree! You are doing something, you say? Yes: producing leaves and casting a shadow! And that is not enough by any means. Christ wants more; he wants fruit. If your honesty, your loyalty, your justice and your sanctity are not greater than those of the scribes and pharisees, you will not enter into the kingdom of heaven. How can you be so ignorant of the demands that Christ makes on his followers? It is clear that you have not gone very deeply into the tasks that we have to fulfil down here on earth.

It is no use looking around you at others; you personally are asked for sanctity. Perhaps this idea of sanctifying yourself, of becoming a saint, had never entered into your plans?

Precisely what God asks of us all is sanctity. And he asks you specifically to sanctify yourself in the world, without leaving it. From all eternity he thought of you as sanctifying yourself in the state of matrimony, with that very wife or that husband, and those very children. And is it possible now that you are ignorant of God's will? We all know something of the effort, the strength and the courage that are needed to reach the heights that he expects of us. But at least be aware of what his will is for you, do not just ignore it as you are doing, make an effort to achieve it, do something about it.

One of those many millions of people that are all around us in the world, wrote the following: 'You speak to me of sanctity and perfection in my ordinary life, and I like to hear you speak in that way. But you are very different from me. I am a married man, I have a wife and family to look after and think about. As well as that, my work takes up many hours every day, because if I am to run my home properly I have to work hard. Of course I try to be honest and just and to fulfil my religious duties. What more can God ask of me? What more can I do for him?'

I think there are many others who might be willing to add their signatures to that letter! So many people who think they know something! So many blind men who are proud of how well they think they can see! And what about you: would you sign that letter?

I can hear you saying: 'My circumstances are peculiar. I have no . . . ' Go on, finish the sentence. You have no time for sanctity: is that what you were going to say? You thought that sanctity was a question of time. Time for what? Time to waste in acts of piety?

You are married and you fulfil your religious duties; what more can God expect of you? If, as you say, you are really honest and just, what you must do is to open your eyes and try to see and understand once and for all what the Lord asks of us Christians.

When are you going to realise what God wants of you now, in that concrete situation in which you find yourself? Or are you one of those who are waiting for some change in their position before starting out seriously along the right path? Let us not fool ourselves like the schoolboy who puts off his study with the excuse that he will begin next Monday, when today is only Tuesday! We are like a child who decides to leave the hard work until 'after the Christmas holidays'. Why do we let ourselves be deceived by our own laziness? When the present situation changes! And you think that is a serious excuse? 'When the present situation changes' was also the excuse given to the king by the guests whom he had invited to the wedding feast and who did not want to come. One of them had bought a new field, another a yoke of oxen, a third, like you, had got married. And not one of the three was allowed to enter into the kingdom. You must attend when God calls, and not wait for the circumstances to change.

Later, tomorrow, another time: that is what you say to God, and you leave him waiting like a beggar at the door of your heart.

Later, tomorrow, another time, but not today: as if sanctity depended on the amount of free time at your disposal! As if tomorrow you would find it easier! Why should you? Because you refused to respond today?

> *How many times the angel said to me*
> *'Soul, look out your window now and*
> *You will see with how much love he is calling and calling'*
> *And how often, o sovereign beauty, I answered*
> *'We will open the window tomorrow'*
> *And answered the same tomorrow.*
>
> *(Lope de Vega)[1]*

Tomorrow, tomorrow. And so the years pass by, and you go on postponing your life until tomorrow.

Show clearly, Lord, to those whom you have called to sanctify themselves in marriage the path you want them to follow. Open their eyes that they may see, understand, accept – and not wreck – the plan that you have made for them. You see how stupidly they use the circumstances in which they are living as an excuse for not going to you. Lord, give life and strength to these words of mine, so that those people may realise that the circumstances, the peculiar individual circumstances, in which they are each living at this moment – their status, age, health, way of life, family, work, financial situation, ambitions – are the framework foreseen by you to be used by them, today and now; as an indispensable, vital, perfectly adequate and irreplaceable means to ascend to great heights and, with the dynamic and effective impulse of your grace, to come to an understanding of sanctity.

Christians, do not spoil your life with your unrealistic and cowardly sighs of 'I wish . . . ' These are the sad and useless laments of the defeated.

'If only I had children' says he who, by God's will, has none. 'If only I had fewer children' says another, who was generous some years ago but has now become selfish and comfort-loving.

'We must finish once for all with that helpless mysticism of "If only . . . "'[2] (Blessed Josemaría). With all this putting off until tomorrow and wishful thinking, your life is slipping through your fingers. 'Tomorrow' and 'when the circumstances change' are excuses, pretexts, in which the sick of spirit take refuge in order to give up the struggle.

Again you ask me: What more can I do for God in my present situation? And again I answer: Make full use of that very situation, for it is no more and no less than a manifestation of God's will for you. You will find him waiting for you precisely in the difficulties of having children, in the problems of supporting and especially educating them, in your ordinary work, in that 'overtime' you have to do, in your tiredness and your exhaustion. And he is waiting for you there today, not tomorrow; now, not later. That is how you must became a saint.

Matrimony is a sacrament by which you receive grace, God's powerful aid, not only for the day of the wedding, but for the whole of your married and family life. So no one can ever say that the opportunity of sanctifying himself is gone; only the dead can no longer merit.

The grace of the sacrament of matrimony is active in every situation throughout the whole of the parents' life, sanctifying them, perfecting their conjugal love and confirming its indissolubility. So there, in your own home, in each unimportant event of your family life, you have Christ. There is no circumstance, no occurrence, where you cannot find him.

There are some people who have the audacity to consider that the goodness of the works of God could be improved upon, and they think there are some actions in marriage which are a little dirty and just have to be gone through with. But, in the words of a friend, of mine, 'the divine act of procreating is not merely the satisfaction of an unavoidable necessity. It is not the accidental justification of something which in itself is bad, a justification which has to be paid for by both spouses having to bear with one another for the whole of their lives. This is the devil's conception of matrimony.'

Here are the words of Scripture: 'For thou hast possessed my reins: thou hast protected me from my mother's womb. I will praise thee, for thou art fearfully magnified: wonderful are thy works' (Psalm 138). 'O Lord, how great are thy works! The senseless man shall not know . . . these things' (Psalm 91).

THE HEROISM OF PARENTS

It is useless to wait until tomorrow or after for some heroic opportunity to come along, in order to serve the Lord faithfully. You act as if you were going to serve a God chosen by your own fancy in your own good time. Remember it was he who chose you, and he placed you where you are to serve him with the means which you have at your disposal today.

If you are not anxious to fulfil the will of God, then family life will be an intolerable burden for you; but if you do really want to serve him, then let me tell you the heroism which he asks of you today, and for you there can be no other heroism.

You have a dreadful headache, but Johnny, the eldest, keeps on singing at the top of his voice. The younger ones are at war in the dining room, while one of the inbetweens is throwing a chair about the place. The little girl comes in, and you have to put a ribbon on her hair.

'Stop singing, Johnny; you'll wake the baby.'

'No, Mummy', the eldest answers you, 'he's awake already.'

The girl's ribbon, the screaming, the singing, the baby waking up crying . . . You have to try and impose a little peace and quiet.

'Mummy, there's a knock at the door.'

'Yes, but there's no need to shout. It's probably your father. Go and see.'

'No, it isn't Daddy, it's a man with a bill.'

'Now, what do we need for tomorrow?' You have to think of tomorrow but . . . 'Don't undo her ribbon, Johnny.' Well, you will have to think of tomorrow's meals later, not now. The children must have their baths now. 'Come on, help me bath the baby.'

And your head is aching worse than ever. But when your husband comes in, you manage to cover up all your little pains with a broad smile.

These are little heroic deeds, which everyone can do from time to time, but which, if practised day after day, add up to great heroism; and if this is done out of love, it is called . . . sanctity.

Mothers, do not complain. Here is Saint Teresa's advice: 'The continual moanings which we make about trifling ailments . . . seem to me a sign of imperfection: if you can bear a thing, say nothing about it. When the ailment is serious, it proclaims itself . . . Do not think of complaining about the weaknesses and minor ailments from which women suffer . . . Unless you get rid of the habit of talking about them and complaining of everything (except to God) you will never come to the end of them . . . Learn to suffer a little for the love of God without telling everyone about it.

'In nothing that I have said am I referring to serious illnesses . . . I am thinking rather of those minor indispositions which you may have and still keep going . . . Let us remember our holy Fathers of past days . . . Do you think they were made of iron? . . . Unless we resolve to put up with death and ill health once and for all, we shall never accomplish anything.'

And here is the heroism of a father: a smile on his lips when he comes home in the evening, tired out after a long and tiring day's work, the work of every day.

Here are the heroic deeds of both father and mother genuine friendliness after having to forgive one another some mutual defects and irritations; cheerfulness, after having to put up with little differences of taste, habits, ideas; good humour, in spite of unpleasant incidents and difficulties, in themselves of little significance, but constantly recurring; remaining silent, not complaining, restraining that outburst which would only make the atmosphere in the house even worse; taking no notice of those thousand and one little annoying details that crop up in daily life. That is the heroism you both have to practise: a heroic epic made up of tiny pinpricks.

There you have the will of God clearly shown to you. There you have Christ waiting for you in the eyes of your children. 'Everything in which we poor men have a part – even sanctity – is a fabric of small trifles which, depending upon one's intention, can form a magnificent tapestry of heroism or of degradation, of virtues or of sins.'[3]

I know that all these pinpricks may at times make your poor heart feel like a pin-cushion. And I also have a feeling that on occasions the pins may be piled up on top of contempt and animosity and then they fall down suddenly, like sharp swords, with treacherous force on your wounded feelings. But on these occasions the Lord's aid will not fail you, that aid which he promised you when you received the sacrament. 'It may be a question of respecting the purposes of marriage as intended by God, or of resisting the burning and attractive temptations of passion or anxiety which entice a troubled heart to seek elsewhere what it has not found in lawful wedlock or what has not fully satisfied its expectations. It may be that, to avoid breaking or loosening the bond of the spirit or of mutual love, one comes to know how to forgive or forget an argument, an insult or even a grave shock' (Pius XII).

When faced with a grave or sorrowful situation you are not asked to smile. But you are asked to raise your eyes to heaven. God expects of you – and it is never above your strength – that heroic act which will end up with eternal joy in heaven, above the stars, while here on earth your children will arise and proclaim you blessed.

Face the future heroically.

Mother, father, you have no cause to be sad, for you will be blessed. You have behaved well. Your sacrifices, your many sacrifices, have passed unseen by our eyes. But God, the good Father of us his children, who sees all, will give you your reward.

[1] Translated by Douglas Mellor.

[2] Sp: *la socorrida mística de la 'hojalata'.*

[3] Bl Josemaría Escrivá de Balaguer, *The Way,* 826, Scepter, Chicago and Dublin, 1964.

7

BEFORE SPEAKING TO YOUR CHILDREN

INFLUENCE AND EXAMPLE

> *The education of children begins about twenty years before their parents are born!*

Parents who consider themselves to be good teachers usually talk too much. Twenty five per cent of the 'advice' they give would usually be quite sufficient, and in some cases this could beneficially be reduced to the still more tolerable figure of one per cent.

A certain boy discovered what I was writing about in my office, so he came and said to me: 'Be sure to tell them that we are fed up with their "experience".' We can be sure that that boy has one of those fathers who try to 'teach' and who talk too much!

Do you not realise that you talk far too much? As if the children's education were in proportion to the number of words you spoke! But in fact the little seed that is to yield fruit in due course makes no noise at all when it falls on the ground: remember that!

Here are some of the things – among many others – which you should never say, even if up to now you have been saying them hundreds of times a day. Indeed, for that very reason it is time to stop now.

A mother should never say: That child of mine has the same bad temper as his father! And a father should never say: That child of mine has the same bad temper as her mother!

Neither parent should say: Put on your coat, take off your coat, be careful crossing the street, stay quiet, don't be so quiet, eat slowly, eat up quickly, I have told you a thousand times, when you are older, tell auntie how old you are, show auntie what the dog does. One woman said to me while her husband was actually listening: 'I am putting this boy in your hands, so that he will grow up to be a bit better than his father.'

This kind of thing would drive anyone mad. Here is a true story: the mother was continually scolding her poor child: 'Stop pulling the chair, you're annoying your uncle; go and play in the garden, you're annoying your uncle; leave that alone, you're annoying your uncle.' Until someone who was there heard the young rascal say: 'I wish uncle would just drop dead!'

A boy told me once: 'They call me five times at home every morning, but the last gives me plenty of time to get to school. The other four have no effect on me.'

Do not speak so much; you are always preaching, and it has become terribly boring. Christ is the best educator that men have ever had, and he spent nine tenths of his life in a little carpenter's shop at Nazareth without saying anything to us in words.

Of course at the extreme opposite, which, is equally dangerous, we find careless parents who completely neglect their duty to direct the shaping of their children's lives. These parents must try to realise that children know nothing, they have to learn everything. Perhaps the only thing they know when they come into this world is how to drink their mother's milk. And it is just as well that nature is wise enough to endow them with this instinct because if they had to wait until they were taught it, some would surely die of hunger.

But that is not the danger in your case. What is wrong with you is that you are too talkative; you have too much faith in your sermons. There are many things you want to, and should, tell your children, but, please, before speaking, let them learn from your life.

You give advice, warnings, threats, prohibitions, stories with a moral – as if children learned only with their ears. You are so anxious to teach, and yet you forget that children learn with their ears, their mouth, their nose, their feet, their hands and their eyes, especially with their eyes. We began to learn when we were born, and we did so just as naturally as we began to breathe. We learned by imitating, from suggestions made to us, quite unconsciously, by our parents' example and influence.

In the period from the time we began to walk on our two feet to the day we first went to school we learned more than in any other period of the same length in our life. Then we continued to learn by watching their life closely.

Sooner or later we began to see into the kind of life they were living, and in that way they did us a lot of good or a lot of harm. My own parents did me a lot of good: may God reward them for it. For instance, for years I was convinced that my mother loved to eat the heads of our favourite fish. How stupid I was, and how slow in waking up to the fact that what that good mother loved was not cod's head but her children. She wanted us to have it all.

But there are other parents, many others, whose way of life cannot but be noticed by their children and it does them very much harm in their head, in their heart, in their poor ideals. Whatever a child sees or feels goes straight into his mental make-up; it creates his personality and remains with him all through his life.

I must say I was very touched by a story I heard from a primary school teacher – and, by the way, is there any more difficult vocation than that of a primary school teacher? She moved me very much when she told me the excuse given by a child of six when he arrived at school one morning: 'Don't ask me the lesson today, Miss, because my father came home drunk last night and he wouldn't let me study or sleep.'

Parents, if you do not teach your children properly by your good example, then there is no point in your weeping for Christ as he painfully and joyfully goes up the hill of Calvary. Weep not for him, but for yourselves and for your children, whom you are trying to take with you to a hell of misery.

Those parents who do their best to live in accordance with the demands the Lord makes on them and who, by their lives, teach their children to do the same, will be called great in the kingdom of heaven. Jesus explained to his disciples what they were to do in the world, after he had told them what they were to be. For 'every prophet who teaches the truth, if he do not what he teaches, is a false prophet' (*The Didache*). 'We base our religion, not on making speeches, but on teaching and giving example by deeds' (Athenagoras).

I have much more confidence in silent but saintly parents than in preachers and orators who fail to practise what they preach. If you want to teach your children to live a Christian life, then you will have to behave as the fathers of families did in the second century. For those men had the spirit of Christ living in them: 'They do not proclaim in the multitude the kind deeds they do, but are careful that no one should notice them; and they conceal their giving just as one who finds a treasure and conceals it. And they strive to be righteous as those who expect to behold their Messiah, and to receive from him with great glory the promises made concerning them' (Aristides). A little further on we read in this same text: 'Truly blessed is the race of the Christians, more than all other men on the face of the earth.'

You must give example, yes, but – please – you must not set yourself up as an example; that would be gross presumption. You are not meant to put on an act. To give example is not, in itself, to be the motive of your actions. Do not try to appear bad; but neither must you *pretend* to be good. You must, quite simply, *be* good.

It is no use trying to go to Church more often than your next-door neighbour. It is little use doing in front of your children something you would not do if you were alone. It is no use giving your good example in that pharisaical way.

Your children are interested in your life. They will be influenced and affected by all your fears, social prejudices, scruples, lusts, attachments, likes and dislikes, manias, grudges, superstitions; they will be influenced and affected by your big lies and your little lies. All those sentiments, noble or base, lofty or petty, radiate outwards and become as it were 'family sentiments'. If you know a child, you can know exactly what his parents are like.

If you are tyrants, your children will be either rebels or men of no personality.

If you are unyielding, they will be hypocrites.

If you are distrustful, they will be timid.

If you spoil them, they will be irresponsible.

If you have little faith, they will be superstitious.

If you have little hope, they will be childless.

If you have little love, they will be envious.

If you do not love freedom, they will be servile.

If you preach what you do not practise, they will be pharisaical.

If you are misers, their heart will be in money.

If you are scrupulous, they will be obsessed with impurity.

If you are individualistic, they will be useless in the fight to save the world.

How unfortunate, how unhappy, you will make your children, if they see that you are the first in leaving God's commands unfulfilled.

It is good to remind your children that they must keep their word like Regulus. Tell them the story of that great Consul, but do not be so naive as to think that because they listen to you quietly they are going to do what you say. 'Two totally different psychological processes are confused', says Foerster. 'First, the child's interest in the action and situations described in the story and, second, his interest in imitating these actions . . . By means of a plastic exposition of lofty acts, the child's volitional energy is never aroused, unless the gap is bridged to the individual circle of his life and ideas; that is to say, unless the corresponding modes of action which are recommended to the child are translated concretely in terms of his infantile motivations and unless every-day events and situations are related to the natural action and will of the child.'

Now I want to ask you: are you yourself faithful to your word? If not, then stop telling them stories, because they will learn only to be faithful and honest like you – they will learn only to ignore the obligations they undertake when they pledge their word.

You want to know when you are most giving example? – When you think you are completely alone with your thoughts. You teach much more when you are not trying to teach, than when you put on a serious face and frown and set out to give lessons. When you come home from work, when you leave down the newspaper to talk to them, when you are having meals with them, when you pray, when you get down on your hands and knees and play with them, when you smile with your lips but your eyes show that you are worried about something, when you do not boast and look for compliments, when you refuse to be downhearted by others' jealousy, then, when you are least concerned with teaching your children, they think to themselves: I want to be like my father.

It is easy to worry about the dangers of the cinema; it is easy to complain about the bad influences at work on your child once he leaves the house; it is easy to blame 'nowadays' – which is so shocking! – for everything. But listen to this: 'Following the principles of modern psychology, competent Catholic educationalists in some countries have conducted detailed enquiries into the religious life of students, especially during their adolescent years. If we are to accept their findings, a rather startling conclusion has been arrived at: that the danger caused by the movies in undermining the faith of our young people is less grave than that which could stem from possible defects and failings of the priest and of teachers and educators in general . . . What a powerful reminder of your responsibilities!' (Pius XII).

Yes, parents; every defect of yours does great harm to your children, because for them you represent the best in life. However, there is no need to be frightened: they are also influenced by your great love, your uprightness, integrity, dignity, loyalty, sincerity, love of freedom, cheerfulness and serenity, your constancy and peace. They are influenced by all your great ideals.

That is the legacy you leave them. Even if you hide your good deeds from them, they – with the right that children have to rummage in their parents' pockets – will come to know your faith, your hope and your charity. Nor is there any point in trying to pretend that you have no defects. You have defects, and your children see them. But they love you with all your faults, just as you must love them . . . just as God loves you.

THE DEVIL'S TEACHING METHODS

Can anything be more monstrous than that a child should obey his father out of fear?

You are rigid, cold, hard, far too authoritarian and serious. So it is only natural that your children never speak to you about their little problems. They have got into the habit of stopping their games abruptly the moment they hear you come into the house, because they are afraid of you. They know it annoys you to hear even a little noise coming from the play room.

When you come home from your work, the way you say 'good evening' shows there is a storm brewing. The youngest child is watching you closely. You hide at once behind the big newspaper pages, but through them the little fellow can imagine the same face he knows so well. Unlike you, he is quite happy. Since he returned from school he has been waiting to tell you the big story, the big event of his afternoon. – If you could only have seen him; all the others cheered him; no one could have done it as well as he did! His imagination runs wild.

'Daddy must have heard something about it before he came home', he says to himself. 'It is probable, because all my pals were speaking about it. Maybe he knows about it but is just pretending. Still, perhaps he hasn't heard, because he has acted just the same as every other day: he came in and took up the newspaper. Why doesn't he say something to me?' And the child decides to interrupt you with an 'Ahem', while pretending to look at the picture on the wall farthest from the armchair where you are sitting. Slowly he turns his smiling eyes towards you, but . . . you go on barricaded behind the newspaper walls.

So he taps gently with his little finger on that formidable barrier. You look out from behind the pages, say 'Hello', and then go back to your reading. Then the child shouts: 'Daddy, do you know what I did in school to-day?' And when he begins to tell you all about the great event, with gestures and gesticulations, you cut him short, but without even looking up from the page:

'There is no need to shout. I can hear you.'

Then there is deep silence. If you only looked at the child's eyes at the moment you could read clearly: 'No, you can't hear me, you are not even listening. You are more interested in the big black words in the paper than in my great deed at school.' And slowly, with his eyes fixed on his enemy the newspaper, he backs away to the door and goes silently to the play room.

The child bears no grudge, and he will quickly forget the way you have ignored him this evening. But if these hurtful incidents continue. you cannot expect him to keep you informed about his sports activities and much less about those little pinpricks of curiosity that have been troubling his imagination for some time past. If he speaks of them at all, it will be to the babysitter, and although she may at times pay no attention, sometimes at least she will listen to everything he tells her about school. She then, and not you his parents, will be friend and adviser.

If you are not interested in his affairs, how can you expect him to be interested in yours? Why should he? Why are you so unjust with your children? Of course in that way, as a cold, hard, rigid man, you will have a much quieter life. No one will play jokes at table. You will speak and everyone will listen to you. But any advice you give will have no effect. They will obey your rules, not as something of their own to be loved, but as a burdensome imposition to which they have to resign themselves if they want to go out playing on Sunday.

It is worthwhile telling you, in her own words, a certain woman's child experience, a little tragedy that happened to her at the age of four. 'My sisters spent the whole day at school, so they were not there. I was alone in the garden, near the house, and I just happened to pick up a little branch of a tree. As I rubbed it between my fingers the bark fell off and I was left with a little wand that had all the appearance of ivory. I was delighted with this new thing, and such a beautiful thing, in my hand. I rushed breathlessly into the room where my mother was talking to Miss Corner. Quite delighted, I exclaimed: "It is me who have done it!" They did not even raise their heads. But governess, with her usual stern voice, corrected my grammar

'I did it', she said.

I said nothing. She became impatient.

'Say: "I did it".'

With my head down and completely despondent, I still remained silent.

'Will you please repeat that? Children are so stupid.'

That was the only time my mother slapped me.

The magic wand seemed broken and disenchanted in my trembling hand' (Jean Vieujean).

Parents, you must be interested in your children. If you show interest in their ivory wands, they will show interest in improving their grammar.

Gone are the days, and not to be regretted, when parents occupied a regal position in the house, up on a throne far too lofty to give audience to the mere desires of their offspring. You must be on a level with your children. Up on your throne you will get a lot of respect, certainly, but very little friendship; yes, a lot of respect and a lot of fear.

Many lamentable things can happen in the education of children; there have always been difficult points. But can anything be more monstrous than that a child should obey his father because he fears him? Afraid of his father! Afraid of a teacher! Afraid of a superior! Afraid of the world! Afraid of God! These are all attitudes that stem from the same erroneous educational method. It is an education in slavery, in unfriendliness, that no parent wants to give and yet everyone seems to get; that no one advocates and everyone learns. The devil must be very happy about all this! His educational methods have triumphed!

Allow no fears, no phobias, to enter your home. Fears – just like Pilate's fear of becoming involved, and like the fear the Gerasenes had of the supernatural (cf Luke 8, 37) – end up in treachery. The only fear you should allow into your family is the gift known as fear of the Lord, and this means being afraid, not of God, but of sin. Become young again; come down from the high pedestal of your thirty or forty years and stay at the level of your children. Show interest in their affairs; try to think as they think, try to understand their ambitions, live their life, return their affection.

An upbringing based on confidence and friendship will bring your children to confide in you and regard you as their friend. And to become their friend should be your first step in educating them. You are a friend who is older than they, has had more experience, more love; a friend who never lies; a friend who corrects with a mere inflexion of the voice, without shouting, with a gesture that no one else will notice; a friend that the children can play with, because he knows their games, their pleasures, their scale of values; a friend who forgets himself and leaves down the paper to hear the latest news that the child brings from school; a friend who gives all his attention to the little girl of four who brings a treasure to show him, even if it is only a little stick that looks like ivory.

They will forget, in time, everything you taught them in talks and on walks; but one idea, one clear, precise and helpful idea they will remember: that their parents were their best friends.

KNOW, UNDERSTAND AND TRAIN THEM

It seems you cannot understand your children. You give them all the same food, the same example, the same teaching; they all live in the same family atmosphere and, nevertheless, they all react in a different way, each one with a different attitude.

That, my dear parent, is quite natural. You must get rid of the idea that all your children should be equal. God himself has made them different; each soul is a work of art fashioned by the love of God. Each child is a world to himself, he has his intellect, his will, his character and characteristics, his virtues and his defects; he has all the qualities and elements necessary for him to develop his own individual personality.

The difficult art of bringing up children consists in understanding each one of them and helping them to develop and exercise all the faculties that God has given them. There is nothing strange or unusual in a very active and hard-working father having a son who is indecisive, small-minded and sentimental, or a daughter who thinks only of sport and going for walks. You must expect to find at times great differences of character among your children, but there will always be some resemblances confirming the bonds of blood. It is wrong of you to try and treat them as if they were poured out of the same mould, made to a pattern.

'Each child dictates the direction he will take and sets his own pace. If the shepherds try at all costs to lead the whole flock at the same pace, to use the same incitements or the same whip, then the number of stragglers, of wounded and of deserters, will soon show them the mistake they have made' (Le Gall).

You have to accept and love each child as he is: brilliant, intelligent, bright, normal or dim, as the case may be.

It is the first child that upsets the mother most. It is all so new to her. But there is no need to be worried when the one-year-old, who can just drink from a cup, use a spoon and toddle around on all fours, first takes off his socks to go to bed, and then puts them on again! This does not seem a bit funny to you at the time, although in fact it is quite funny. Older mothers laugh when they think back on these first experiences.

You must be patient when the baby cries. Learn, as soon as you can, to distinguish between when he is crying just to be petted and when it is that he wants to be changed. If you cannot let your child cry when there is nothing wrong with him, you will become a slave of his childish whims. He is not stupid, you know, and he quickly learns to relate his crying with your attention, and so he uses his tears as a bell. Well, let him ring the bell, but do not answer. If you do not put this advice into practice with your first child, experience will make you do so with your third or fourth!

Do not be upset by the definite 'no' you constantly get from the child of two. It means he is at the 'contrary' stage, which is not unusual in a child's development. This is the awakening of the will; it manifests itself in stubbornness, which is found in all children and not just in yours. You yourself also went through that 'negative' period.

Before they reach the age of two, there is no point in trying very hard to tell them stories: at that age they will not listen. But later on, they will; tell them stories then and they will be delighted. You are mistaken if you think there are more important things to do than telling your children stories. And I mean stories with no moral, just stories, nothing artificial; stories just to make them laugh, to cheer them up, to amuse them.

I have a friend who invented a character for the stories he tells his children. He is a good giant called Bumble. And the children come to him and say: 'Today you must tell us about Bumble when he went skiing.' Then my friend's imagination goes on location to the woods covered in snow.

If the father is very unimaginative, then the mother will have to tell the stories. If neither of you has any imagination, then you will have to buy storybooks and read them to the children.

At the age of three they simply cannot stay quiet for a moment. I would go even further and say they should not stay quiet. Their development does not allow it; they need movement, for this is the age of action and they become completely dynamic. This is the time when they acquire most valuable experience: they run, jump, climb, and ride their tricycle. They are in continuous movement and they make everyone else in the house follow suit.

Take care of them at that age. A child of less than three has no sense of danger. He is more interested in the ball that bounces out into the street than in all the cars that are passing. A child of that age cannot yet restrain certain impulses, however obedient and docile he may be.

There is no need to worry too much about the knocks and bumps. These are the first of many lessons in curious experimental knowledge that they will get throughout their life. But never again do what you did this morning. The child bumped into the table and got a good knock on the head. Then the father, the mother, the aunt, the grandfather – especially the grandfather – every one of you, to console the child, hit the table and shouted: 'Bad table'. No, that is not the right thing to do. The table is not bad. It is the child who is stupid – I mean, careless.

To understand your child is to feel your way into his private fantastic world.

You insisted on explaining to your little daughter that the beautiful train engine you had brought her was the most expensive toy you could find. But the girl paid no attention to you and went on playing with her doll, which now consisted only of a big head and a pointed nose. You have no poetry in your soul! You failed to see that the little girl could add nothing to that beautiful engine, while the doll depended on her for everything. You understand? It depends on her. She puts on its clothes, its bright red clothes, she takes it for a walk, sings to it, puts in its eyes which make it look beautiful, decorates it with golden hair that reaches down to its feet. The head is no longer a head; it is a fairy going and coming to the castle, bearing her long silky train. Everything about that faded but fantastic doll's head is wonderful.

You were hurt by the child's unintentional rejection of your present. I said you must feel your way into that world of fantasy. And how could you hope to feel your way in there with a train engine? That is a blatant intrusion. I am not surprised that today she has closed the gates of her private world and left you outside.

That is not the end of the development. The age of action, around the age of three, is followed by the age of investigation and inquiry, which comes around four. While the child could not speak, he watched, listened, smelled, felt and let others live as they liked. But when he learns to speak you must live for him. Two hundred 'whys' a day and three hundred 'hows' will be very exhausting if you are not prepared for them. You may find yourself wishing he could always be as quiet and kissable as he was during his early years. In these cases, you must never get into bad humour, whatever you do. The children will bring joy into your saddest days with their smiles, their glances, their kisses, their good humour.

'Won't it be great fun, Daddy,' says a mite of five looking at his sixth little sister in her cradle, 'when there are fourteen of us!'

Do not lose your patience at their spontaneous outbursts; these do not show any malice, but are only part of the fantastic novel they are living all the time. On one occasion a father was trying to explain to his sons a picture that showed some of the first martyrs being eaten by wild beasts. He was trying to tell the child how those first Christians were clawed to pieces by the lions. He was hoping for a reaction of pity, but he was disappointed. The child was much more attracted by the lions than by our brothers the early Christians, and he burst out: 'Look, Daddy, this poor lion has no Christian to eat' (Courtois).

Unless you are acquainted with the world of your children, you may suffer grave disappointments. Like that lady who, quite wrongly, mistook for impoliteness what was mere naturalness on the child's part. She was in a reception room waiting for the owners of the house, when the youngest member of the family came in on hands and knees, jumped about a little on the carpet and then began to go out again. The lady stopped him: 'Are you the youngest of the family? What's your name?' And with great naturalness he answered without raising his head, for he had no interest in visitors: 'I'm a cow.'

The child of three or four likes to comb his hair, wash his face, brush his teeth. Often at four or five he can take a bath without any help, although he still likes to play with the soap. Do not scold him for the few minutes he wastes playing. For you soap is something which you use merely to wash your hands; and that is because you look at it from above. The child looks at it from a different angle; for him it is a very interesting thing that produces bubbles. And with all those bubbles around, what else is there of interest?

Soon he can dress himself without any help. The dreadful thing is to see a child of eight or nine – and it is you parents who are to blame for this – being helped to dress by a soft, doting mother. And another thing: why not let the child himself decide what he is going to wear? Get him used to looking out of the window when he gets up in the morning to see what clothes he should put on: overcoat, cap, raincoat or pullover. How do you intend teaching him to be responsible? Give him responsibilities, from a very early age, in material things.

I am not exaggerating when I give you this definition written very recently by a good-humoured boy in a school exercise: 'A pullover is a thing that a boy has to wear when his mother feels cold.'

If he wants to eat without your help, let him. Why should you try to disturb that new experiment, that exciting exercise? To do things well, he must first do them badly, so do not scold him. Encourage him when he is doing it well, praise his little successes. And do not be irritated by his little failures, even if they do make the place dirty. This is inevitable. You look at everything with the eyes of an adult, and that is what you must not do: you must see them with the eyes of a little child.

If your little daughter likes to lay and clear the table, let her do it. And there is no need to shout: 'Be careful, don't break anything', because she will not break anything. What you should do is show her the order in which she must do the different things.

I mentioned already that children have to learn everything, that they inherit very little knowledge and have to acquire the vast majority by habit. And this does not refer exclusively to habits of manners, cleanliness or neatness. Habit may also teach them to think, to feel, to have good taste. Someone said that even one's attitude to life is, to a certain extent, a question of habit. And it is clear that children learn to be either cheerful and happy or bad-humoured and gloomy according to the habits they acquire. The majority of their habits are acquired in the first four years of their life and, once acquired, they are never forgotten.

With this in mind, remember that they can understand perfectly the idea of God being present everywhere. So, get them to live 'presence of God'.

On the other hand, do not ask them to make resolutions for the day after tomorrow, because the day after tomorrow has no meaning for children. They live in a perpetual 'today and now'. At the very most, 'later' may go as far as bedtime, but no further.

Children are nourished by food and sleep. So, get them to have order in these things, and do not allow them to indulge their whims at the wrong times. Give them a little plan of life. Idleness is as harmful and perverse in children as it is in grown-ups; it is when they are bored that things always go wrong. They need to have a fixed time to eat, to dress, to play, to sleep, to put their toys in order, to go for a walk. Without order they will never acquire good habits.

How can you expect them to be anything but riotous and fond of pandemonium if one day you make them dress before having breakfast and the next day you let them have it in pyjamas? They will be at a loss to know which is right.

Teach them responsibility. Up to the age of six you had to think only about the child and the home, or at most about sending him to kindergarten; but from the age of seven you will have to start thinking of the child, the home, the school he goes to, the street he plays in, the friends he has, the books he looks at, the foreign languages he learns. Things begin to get a bit complicated!

I don't want to speak about sports, because I think you are fully aware of the need for them. What I do want to remind you – because you may forget these things –

is that about the age of seven is probably the best time to begin to learn a foreign language; that if a child of ten asks for a little corner of the house for himself or at least a drawer, he should be given it; that you should take an interest in his interests, and get him to have many, so that he will have at least one worth carrying on in later life. They should all have some interest or hobby, and you should encourage them: music, painting, mountain-climbing, hunting, fishing and the whole range of manual hobbies. I shall have more to say of this later.

You can be sure of bringing them up properly if you keep in mind constantly that the function of good parents is to become unnecessary as soon as possible. The parents' whole endeavour should follow this line: that the children should be got as soon as possible into a position where they can act for themselves. I believe that this sense, this spirit, of responsibility is the thing that really matters in a man.

Those parents who, through mistaken understanding of love, try to take on themselves all the dangers, worries, difficulties and even illnesses that come the way of their children will make them incapable of facing up to life. But enough of this subject, until we come to speak of controlling and spoiling children.

Somewhere between the attitudes of those parents who never intervene, who want only to be left in peace, and those others who repeatedly punish their children for mere trivialities, is the ideal attitude, the attitude you must adopt.

The punishment which will help a child to acquire the habit of responsibility is one which is directly related to the action that is being punished. A punishment must always be reasonably proportionate to the fault and never a way of working off bad humour.

If a child breaks a toy, it is a good punishment to deprive him for a few days of the use of other toys. It is a good and pedagogically sound punishment to make a child who has deliberately and maliciously broken a pane of glass, get it repaired, or at least to pay for it by instalments out of his savings.

This must all be done without creating any of those 'scenes' which are so common with 'loving', but overexcitable, mothers. There is no need to raise your voice when delivering a scolding or punishment. And if a child shouts, be sure to speak to him in a low calm voice.

He should not be afraid of his parents, even when they punish him. If the punishment is inflicted without love it will have an effect while the fear lasts, but it will be of no avail in transforming the child's interior disposition.

Do not punish at all if you are angry; wait until you are calm again. Otherwise you will be unfair. 'Wait until the next day, or even longer. And then, calmly, and with a purer intention, make your reprimand. You will gain more by one friendly word than by a three-hour quarrel' (*The Way*, 10).

As I understand it, punishment should be given calmly, tactfully, opportunely, clearly, reasonably, without trying to humiliate, without being absurd, to the degree of sending a boy of twelve to bed for the whole of a Sunday afternoon. Perhaps unthinking mothers will see no danger even in this.

Sometimes, but very seldom, a slap may be the most effective remedy. But in my opinion this is a right, exclusive to parents, which they should exercise only seldom, and certainly never in the case of their daughters.

After punishment, forget the offence. You must go back immediately to the friendly relations that existed before.

Do not threaten punishments that you have not thought out carefully, because if the offence you have warned against is committed, you then have no alternative but to impose the punishment.

Avoid the mistake of that poor teacher, who was terribly bad-tempered and went on increasing the amount of punishment according as the pupils, completely in control of themselves and of the situation, enjoyed watching his rising temper.

'Two days without recreation.'

A slight smile in the back row.

'Five days' detention.'

A little whispering from the class forced the raging teacher to raise his voice:

'Fifteen days.'

Then the contest began between their laughs and his anger, and from the start it went in favour of the pupils.

'Twenty . . . fifty . . . eighty days without recreation.'

And as he increased the number of days, as if counting his money, the pupils' laughter grew louder and louder, ending up in a loud guffaw when the teacher, having reached the enormous number of four hundred days' detention, stalked out of the room, and banged the door behind him.

A child should be trained to eat everything and to complain about nothing. But if he is to acquire that habit, the child needs parents who complain about nothing and eat everything too.

Standing beside a child who was sick in bed, his mother said to me: 'Tell him that grapes are very good for him; he doesn't believe it.' I did so, and you can imagine my shame a few days later when that boy told me that his mother had contracted the same illness and was refusing to eat the grapes the doctor had prescribed for her!

If the children prefer to stay in the house, when there are visitors (just to be with their mother, in the world of grown-ups), then they are too closely tied to her apron strings, they are becoming weaklings. Send them out to play! The child must live in his own world, the world of children. That is where he can speak out with authority; that is where he can learn to judge and make decisions.

You ask me if you should give them some pocket-money. Of course you should! Why should you think of neglecting that aspect of their training in responsibility? They must learn to be neither misers nor spendthrifts. You teach them the middle way by letting them handle money. Would you like to be the parent of that boy who came to me and said: 'You are a good friend of my parents; why don't you tell them to give me some money, so that I won't have to steal it from them every Sunday?' It is just as dangerous to keep the cash-box open to satisfy their every whim, as it is to keep it tightly closed when there are genuine little needs to be satisfied. You should assign them a certain sum – which they should not call their 'pay' – so that they will learn to use money properly.

A little child of six should be given money to buy 'that' definite thing. He is not yet capable of saving up for the future. But a boy of twelve should be in the habit of paying for whatever he wants out of his weekly or monthly allowance: his haircut, bus fares, outings, alms and of course sweets, and also the bulb he broke with the football. He should be free to spend his money as he likes; his expenses and his savings are his own business. You should not do it all for him. But you should take the opportunity of speaking to him about the experience he is having through his contact with money. One thing you should not do is to give him an advance half way through the week because he spent foolishly during the first few days. Let him learn for himself how costly bad management can be.

This question of money, as so many other questions, needs to be well thought out and explained to the children. Education is indeed a difficult thing, remember that; and your vocation is a heroic one.

What about promising money on condition that the school report or examination results are good? This may be a risky business. Used once or twice, I see no harm in it; but to use it always would be very bad. But neither should you keep back their pocket-money because of bad marks. There is no relation between the two; it would be better to make them stay in and study.

Do not use saving as a pretext for cheating your children. I am referring to a kind of deceit of which many of us may have been the victims when we were young. During the year we had been putting our pennies in a money box. Then at last the great day arrived, sometime around Christmas probably, when the box was to be opened and the money counted. We agreed that saving was definitely a good idea: so much money at one time! But then came our disappointment: can you guess what was bought for us with our savings? A pair of shoes!

The parents of a friend of mine enticed him to take his castor oil by putting a penny in his money box for each spoonful. You will never guess what they bought him with the money he had saved by forcing himself to take all those horrible spoonfuls? – Another bottle of castor oil! So at least two of us hate those money boxes.

There are many ways of wasting money on children. Here are some examples: buying a boy a bicycle as soon as he can ride one, because he passes one examination; buying him a motor cycle the moment he reaches the legal age because he passes another examination; buying him an expensive gold-topped pen, the latest imported model, so that he can lose it and have to buy a cheap ballpoint.

Among the good ways of spending money I would mention sending them to a good school. They need sound education and a wide culture. You must be very ambitious in this matter, like the mother of the sons of Zebedee who asked for the two highest posts in the kingdom for her sons; and Jesus, who was very hard on selfishness, was quite patient with that woman. The least you can do is make sure they are being taught languages. Another good use of money is to tear up into little pieces or throw away all the money they have saved, if you see that they are turning out to be misers.

If a child does not know how much it costs to send a letter abroad or to send a postal order or a parcel, if he has never paid a bill, or does not know the price of the shoes he is wearing or the overcoat his parents are going to buy him, then it is clear that they have neglected to give him what they should have given him: a strong sense of responsibility.

With an American author, I can tell you that girls of between ten and twelve years old are capable of preparing not only a well planned but also an inexpensive meal. And it is a pleasure for them to do the shopping for all the day's meals, provided the family recognises their merit and does not forget to praise the dishes they choose.

The girls should be able to serve at table, take their little brothers for a walk, go shopping and, of course, do some housework; and the boys should be able to polish their shoes, mend a fuse, choose their ties, clean their bicycle, wash the dishes, and type.

BE PREPARED

Children grow up! This is quite obvious, of course, but it is something you must keep very much in mind, because parents too often forget it and they are nearly always behind in recognising the development of their children. They still call them 'babies' when they are children, they call them 'children' when they should be called boys and girls, and they call them 'boys and girls' when they are men and women.

Have you never seen parents fly into a rage just because their children begin to speak of marriage at an age . . . at which they themselves got married? It is little things like this that cause so many conflicts between parents and children.

Anyway, children grow up and, sooner or later, reach that age which some call 'ungrateful' and others call 'awkward', but which in any case is a beautiful age . . . laden with heartaches. It is an age that has nothing to do with those that went before it. The girl is becoming a woman and the boy is becoming a man.

You were just beginning really to understand the world of your children; and then you find that the eldest girl has had her twelfth birthday and the eldest boy his thirteenth, and something new has come along, new for you and new for them.

Unless they are prepared for it, this new stage of development will be very unpleasant for parents. Those who are unprepared will want at all costs to maintain the same rights as before: the same authority, the same discipline, the same affection. And the children, without understanding why, feel that they are being victimised; they crave, with all their heart, for freedom and independence. At this stage they want to go out with their friends, and the eldest girl does not like to go out walking with her mother.

This attitude is all very natural. These are just little affirmations of their personality. A mother who is prepared and sensible will gently loosen the strings at the right time. She knows that a few years later, at sixteen, the same girl will ask her to go with her.

If parents are unprepared or nervous, at this stage they try to pry into the minds and souls of their children, just when they tend to close up in themselves. It is when you are most interested in them, because you are worried by their growing up and their romantic notions, and you want to know with whom they are keeping company and where they are going, that you are very disconcerted by their laconic replies: 'I just went for a walk', 'I was out.'

This is the period when an over-jealous mother will suffer, seeing her sons and daughters slipping from between her fingers and being able to find no way of holding on to them. During this period there is something much more important than maintaining parental authority at any cost, something much more important than shouting (which in any case has no effect on them), something much more important than those sentimental outbursts of 'you are causing me endless worry', or 'you are intolerable'. The most important thing at these times is to keep calm. The policy of not interfering immediately is the best and the most advisable.

The phrase 'at all costs' is one you should not utter in front of the children: it will only incite them to rebellion. Supervision – of course – is absolutely essential, but it must be an indirect supervision. This is the time when your common sense can be put to best use. That force, that insistence, which at former stages may have given results now has the very opposite effect.

The girl, who up to now was so hard-working and studious, has become very lazy. The boy, who always took such an active part in sport and games, is now a mere spectator, his bones seem to be too heavy for him to carry. You need not look in his drawer, I can tell you what is in it: stamps, match boxes, comics, bus tickets, football tickets, coloured postcards and pictures, old coins. He begins a new collection every week or two. Encourage him to be orderly and constant.

They spend all their time with their unfinished collections, their poetry, letters, diaries, romantic ideas, reading (which is always a good thing), great affection and equally great disrespect for their parents. And the girls begin their first love affairs; they will tell you about them and keep you informed if you have gained their confidence during the preceding stages.

The time has come when the house is no longer large enough to contain them. If the parents – foolishly – neglected to acquire friends and establish close relations with other families, then they will find that the children go out to be with others who are bound to be unknown to them.

Parents must give their attention to social relationships, for their own sakes and for the sake of their children.

It should not surprise you in the least if your son of fifteen makes great attempts from time to time to be independent in opinion and in action, only to go back to his childish behaviour ten minutes later, as if he were only ten. At this age children are very emotional, sentimental, inconstant, imaginative, sensible and reasonable, with the traits of a mature man and the outbursts of a toddler. The same children who at school behave at times as generous and understanding men, at home may be selfish and disobedient.

They are going through a transition period; and if you loosen the strings they feel insecure, while if you tighten them they feel that they are being victimised.

But, parents, do not despair. You have a greater duty to keep calm than they have, because you cannot expect them to understand themselves at all; they know what they do not want, but they just cannot decide what they want. Biologically and psychologically they are beginning to face life, and all these changes and upsets are perfectly natural.

The behaviour you demand from them in that despotic way of yours – that they should always be docile, always obedient, always submissive, always affectionate, always well mannered, always acting like ladies and gentlemen – frankly, is impossible in a healthy child. And if your children behave like that, then I do not compliment you on it. They are under-developed as regards their will, and they should see a doctor.

You must understand them. You must at least try to understand them.

Loving mothers, now that you feel you are being abandoned a little, now that you feel like begging your children to love you – because naturally you want to be loved by them – remember that this is a time more than ever before when your children, and in a special way your daughters, are in need of affection, understanding, consideration and respect, just now when you see that their young womanly heads are so full of levity, frivolity, stupidity.

Now that their affection for dolls – which they abandoned at the age of ten – has been replaced by an affection for boys of fifteen or sixteen; now that their aesthetic taste is tending towards clothes designed to attract and please; now that money is of no importance compared to their beauty; now, now especially, you must make an effort to understand them. Try to show them that all the world of poetry and sorrow that is opening up before their eyes, all those difficulties that stem from their changeable character, all those fantastic joys and all those frequent depressions that end up in tears, are only the price, and a very cheap price, that our Father God asks of them in exchange for those great things that are taking shape in them.

Mothers, a new sacrifice is asked of you. Once again your children ask of you – but without asking, because tues. They know they should not kill, or steal, or tell lies; but they are not so well informed about the function of life, or money, or truth. They are better versed in attrition than in contrition. They are taught more about the temptations that come from the devil than about all the aid that comes from their Guardian Angel. They know about the dangers of keeping bad company, but they seldom feel, as they should, a deep and Christian concern to help and improve their friends.

Surely you see that what you are doing will smother every great ambition, every holy aspiration they may have. Do you not see tnat they will grow up believing – and what an accursed belief! – that a man is good if he keeps away from everything bad. Look: can you show me anyone who has done anything worth while in life simply by avoiding evil? Do you know any holy person with a motto containing nothing but negatives? Do you think for a moment that Christ came on earth just so that we would avoid sin? No; he came so that we should have life. Perhaps you thought that sanctity meant avoiding breaches of the law of God. Well, you were wrong; for sanctity consists of fulfilling God's law in a positive way.

How many Christians do you think there are today who realise that the vocation of an ordinary Christian is a vocation to apostolate? How many do you think realise that being a Christian brings with it the obligation – and I mean obligation – to carry out apostolate, to take part in it actively, according to their possibilities? Believe me, it is impossible to train your children in the social obligations that Christianity implies by means of negatives and prohibitions. That system would only teach them to be quite pleased with oneself provided one does not actually maltreat the helpless. Do you think it is sufficient to fulfil the works of mercy in a negative sense?

they are too ashamed – to forget yourself and take care of them in their emotional crises. You must take them seriously; they will allow you to make suggestions but not to make jokes.

And there is no need to be afraid if you see your daughter, at the age of puberty, showing an interest in hobbies, tastes and attitudes that are more proper to a boy than to a girl. 'Let us not harbour any fear', says Guarnero. 'These little signs of masculine ways that frighten us so much will not really harm her femininity, but will help her to get over without any silly conceit this period which can be so prone to the emptiest feminine stupidity.'

Adolescence is a difficult but wonderful period, from which children can reap great benefit provided they have someone on whom they rely and to whom they can pour out their mind. If you were their best friends while they were infants, you will be rewarded now by becoming their closest advisers; advisers who are never frightened, never nervous, who listen without giving any sign of unnecessary alarm to the stories of their first love affairs, which are as pure as the love of a mother for her children; advisers who show confidence in the children; advisers who can shut their eyes and overlook many momentary or even serious failures; advisers who have no need to open letters, because their children read them aloud; advisers who force nobody's conscience, because they have taken the trouble to place the children in the hands of their friend the priest; advisers who seldom punish but who always encourage.

Your children need understanding and support from everyone around them. They need friends who are willing to help. They need someone who will explain to them the reasons for all that confusion in their soul and in their heart. They need someone to satisfy all their legitimate curiosity, which, after all, is a sign that they are intelligent beings. They need someone to direct and channel their rebellious notions, their daring outbursts, their youthful indiscretions. They need someone to answer them properly when they shout: Away with everything old!

Now more than ever, parents, you must be young; now that you have reached a mature age, you must make an effort to come down to their level; think back to when you were fourteen, fifteen and sixteen years old. They need you. They need you to tell them the truth about life, about death, about man, about the world, about love and about the straight path they have to follow.

8

SPEAKING OF LIFE, DEATH, LOVE AND THE WAY

SPEAK TO THEM POSITIVELY

The atmosphere in your home should not be laden wi threats or prohibitions; it should be full of a positi content.

If all the prohibitions that some parents impose their children were written on the walls of their hom there would be no room left to hang a picture. But y home must not be like a railway carriage, where eve thing is forbidden, from smoking to leaning out the v dow. The mother who leaves the upbringing of her c dren in the hands of a governess so that she can g and enjoy herself then becomes a mere ticket inspe in the family. 'Mary', she says, in words I copy Courtois, 'go out and see what the children are c and tell them to stop it.'

If you continue with that dreadful habit of const threatening the children as a means of making 'good', you will really make them 'bad' the momen can get away with something without being see punished.

Those parents who accuse their children of telli and being lazy fall into the same educational er their attitude is equally negative. Unless you trus they will become hypocrites.

With a few honourable exceptions, childrer know more about bad manners than about goc ners. Intellectually they know about sins more t

Broadly speaking, the following could form a positive program for your home

More love than fear.

More virtues than sins.

More angels than devils.

More contrition than attrition.

More confidence than fear.

More amusement than boredom.

More encouragement than reprimands.

More incentives than threats.

More rewards than punishments.

More praise than censure.

More ideals than prohibitions.

More cheerfulness than bad humour.

You can slap a child for banging the door and shout at him to close it quietly. But you can also praise him when he closes a door carefully; and the praise will be much more effective, more positive, more formative, more educational and more Christian. It is something he will never forget.

Take a day to try this out and you will be convinced. If you watch a little, you will easily find ten things for which you can praise your children. And ten praises will save you a hundred reprimands.

SPEAKING OF LIFE AND DEATH

We have agreed, I think, that the home should be bright. Now, it will be impossible for you to give your children any light unless you give them some good, strong ideas concerning life, death, love and the straight path.

There is certainly nothing to be afraid of in teaching them about life and death, yet many parents seem to consider it too complicated to explain the beginning of life and too gloomy to speak about the end of life. How long do they think they should wait before giving their children good doctrine? It is very wrong to hide from them the mysteries of life and death . . .

Listen to this shameful passage which I have just read in a book which otherwise gives sound advice: 'It is very difficult to give a satisfactory answer to a child who asks what happens when a person dies. This is one of the cases in which it is not only permissible but advisable that a mother should answer that she is not sure . . . It is not very consoling to tell the child that when he dies he will go to heaven, because a little child dislikes the idea of going to a far-off place where he will be separated from his parents.

'It is more sensible to tell him that probably he will not die, because nowadays children are so well taken care of that they have no reason to worry.

'The idea of being with God is very vague for his mind, which grasps only what he can see and touch.'

So you think, my friend, that the idea of being with God is very vague! Perhaps for pagans it is. If you have no faith, of course it is difficult for you to speak of death to your children, poor pagan children.

I got as far as page 100 of that book without finding the word 'God' even once, and when it is mentioned it is only to tell us that this God of ours is a very vague idea! They have not got the faith, so it is only to be expected that they should be afraid to speak of God. But we Christians, sons and daughters of that great King, we who base our whole spiritual life on our divine filiation, can be afraid neither of God, nor of life, nor of death.

DON'T BE AFRAID TO SPEAK TO THEM

A boy has just been with me in my office. He is a boy whose eyes usually radiate great cheerfulness, but this time he had lost it all; there was no smile on his face, for the eyes of children do not deceive. This time he kept his head down. (By the way, parents, you must realise that children also have problems that worry them, that weigh heavily on their mind.)

Well, this boy had to beat about the bush for a while before coming to the problem, but at last he got to it. And he blurted it out with the bluntness of great disappointment.

'Now I know the whole thing', he said.

I saw at once that he had a lot of things to say. And I was right.

When he had finished, I said to him:

'So you think your parents were committing sins, is that it?'

And his simple 'yes', curt and bitter, pained me deeply.

I saw that we were late, his parents and I. A few minutes in the company of those friends of his who 'knew the whole thing' had been sufficient to make him lose all that respect, all that veneration, all that unquestioning affection children have for their parents.

'His parents were bad people. His parents were sinning.'

My blood absolutely boils when I see that your cowardice in not speaking to your children in time allows them to imagine that you are sinning when you are actually doing what God wants you to do, you who are bound by your vocation to bring forth children. I cannot understand why you are so reluctant to speak to your children about life. Such stupid fear! How can a mother be so naïve! Open your eyes to reality once and for all! Take the advice of so many experts on educational matters. Do you think that your silence or your lies will make of them men strong enough to stand up to this world which is so often dirty?

A few days ago I was giving a lecture to sixty girls of about seventeen who were just finishing secondary school. Now, you will hardly believe me when I tell you that not one of those girls had heard one word from their parents on the subject of sexual education.

Out of pure carelessness and indifference, we are allowing the children to grow up with the idea that there are certain subjects about which they must not speak to their parents. These are subjects, apparently, which are to be spoken about only in the streets, with their friends, when no one is listening. And since the parents say nothing, the children look elsewhere for the answer to their eager curiosity which, after all, is only proper in an intelligent person who is not satisfied with silence or with lies. The stories of babies being found under cabbages or being brought by the stork show the cowardice of a generation that uses fables to avoid the difficulties of giving good sexual education. To refrain from speaking about this subject is quite deplorable.

A misunderstanding of what modesty is, ignorance of the appropriate terminology and insufficient education of the right kind in the parents themselves, resulted in a generation of parents who shelved this problem and left it clouded in a silence that was clearly uneducational and positively deforming. Up to recently, perhaps, if we take these excuses into account, the method of silence may have been merely stupid, but now, since the Church has spoken out, it is a fault and positively blameworthy. When a child's intelligence demands direction and information on these delicate questions, unless he receives it at home he will have to seek it elsewhere: in an illustrated dictionary, in a book on 'gynaecology' or simply in the street. And thus the child – who ceases to be a child long before his parents like to admit it – will be formed 'in a haphazard way, from some disturbing encounter, from secret conversations, through information received from over-sophisticated companions, or from clandestine reading, the more dangerous and pernicious as secrecy inflames the imagination and troubles the senses"[1] (Pius XII).

And remember, parents, that in those cases the information they get will be either entirely false or, even if it is true, will be distorted, because it will be excessively physiological, without any reference to the moral, sentimental or religious aspects, so necessary at this stage in a child's education.

If you neglect to explain to your child what God has done, there will be someone else willing to do so, and then perhaps he will be shown, not only what God has done, but what the devil has done too.

Mother, there is no need to be frightened at bath time, just because your tiny son sees the sexual differences between himself and his little sister. This only means that the child is not stupid. Very young children are entirely void of any malice in regard to their body. Take this opportunity to explain to him in a very natural way that the Child Jesus made little boys and little girls differently. He must not be given the impression that he has asked anything shameful. If you answer simply, without any hint of mystery, the child will be satisfied with your brief answer, just as he is satisfied with the hundreds of other answers you give to his hundreds of questions every day. You must not bring him up to be afraid of or feel any repugnance for sex; but do speak to him of the natural modesty which God wants him to have.

Everything they learn in their chats with you must be natural, healthy and supernatural. What you should do is teach them to regard the world with pure and clean eyes. The following are some of the many points to keep in mind when teaching your sons and daughters:

If they do not ask where babies come from, then go ahead and tell them unasked. I know of one very modern hospital, so modern that it has storks in the garden to avoid all difficulties if the children ask questions.

Tell them where babies come from, and I promise you it will give them a great love for their mother, a great respect for womanhood and a holy pride in themselves. There is no need to wait until they are fourteen to tell them the father's function, and they will then begin to appreciate, naturally and supernaturally, the spark of creative power that God has given to man.

The young girl should know the cause of menstruation and its relation to the sacred duty of motherhood. She should know – because you should explain it to her – that her early maturity accounts for the attraction she feels for boys who are older than she is.

The young boy should be told the cause of those involuntary emissions which he will have at night, and how that function, which should be used exclusively within marriage, plays its part in bringing new lives into the world.

Sexual education is, of course, important for all children, but for those of a sanguine temperament it is absolutely essential. You will have to warn them against masturbation; if you neglect to do this, I wouldn't like to be in your shoes.

Be a little ahead of the physiological changes in explaining to them all the emotional changes they will undergo. It is essential that you get rid of all your fears and prudish inhibitions. Read a book – there are many good ones – and learn the correct vocabulary to use.

It is a monstrosity to be careless in giving your children a correct knowledge of God's works. What do you think will be the outcome of that carelessness? I can tell you this: if you leave these questions to their own judgment, their sexual life will career along ways of blind sensuality and they will approach marriage covered with filthy selfishness, inside and out. Leave it all to their own instincts and they will turn out to be hypocrites. They will pretend to know nothing and will lose all respect for you.

If they see that you warn them hundreds of times against the dangers of catching a cold and yet you never speak about the struggle that faces them in life, they will naturally conclude that the most important thing is to avoid colds while, apparently, with regard to that other matter nothing can be done.

Your children can learn the great principles of life in your own bright home; why then do you prefer that they should learn them from suspect entertainments or from the filth of the street? You have no right ever to say to them: 'You must not speak of those things.' Of those things precisely you must speak!

'Train the mind of your children. Do not give them wrong ideas or wrong reasons for things. Whatever their questions may be, do not answer them with evasions or untrue statements, which their minds rarely accept, but use this opportunity lovingly and patiently to train their minds, which want only to open to the truth and to grasp it with the first ingenuous gropings of their reasoning and reflective powers' (Pius XII).

I was at the back of a church once, in the last bench that had been left vacant by a crowd of schoolboys who filled the rest of the church. A young woman, showing all the signs of maternity, came in and stood beside a pillar. Immediately they began to stare at her. And from staring, they went on to whispering and sniggering at that woman who was going to be a mother. It never occurred to them to make room for her on the bench! I could not hear their comments: I was too far away; but I could guess what they were.

The whole thing made me terribly angry. So I got up, went over to them and simply said very sadly: 'Do not laugh; this lady is going to be a mother.' They looked at me in astonishment and went back to their prayers. But the moment I knelt down the laughing broke out again.

You can be sure that the teacher, who saw me speaking to them, punished 'the whole bench' when they got back to the school. But I would have preferred to punish him, because whose fault was it but his that, at their age, they should laugh at a woman who was going to be a mother?

I wonder what you think of this lesson in sexual education that was given to a group of friends of mine just before they finished school. They were all sixteen or seventeen. The last day of the term, when the school was breaking up, the older ones were called together to be told 'something very important'. They could see that the teacher who came to speak to them was very nervous, but they could not think of the reason. However, they were soon to find out. For, when he was finishing his farewell speech, still very perturbed and nervous, he added, as something of great importance, perhaps as a kind of epilogue to the training the boys had been given during their years at the school: 'Furthermore, you must remember throughout your life that in the streets and bars there are some very bad women.'

I was with them as they were leaving the school. I cannot write their comments. The only thing I can say is that their laughter filled the whole school.

The formation your children must get from you should be gradual but complete. It cannot be done all at once. Sexual education cannot be compressed into one lesson, simply because there is no single or final sexual education. It is not proper to any one age, but has to be given according as the children's healthy curiosity evolves and develops.

That is why the whole of this delicate aspect of your children's education must be based on complete confidence and friendship built up between you and them. If a child cannot take the newspaper out of the hands of his father when he comes home from school – and this, of course, is the father's fault – how can he possibly have the courage to ask him where children come from?

I am not suggesting that this kind of education is a panacea that will cure all ills, but I am convinced that it will avoid many sexual misadventures that could have deplorable consequences; I believe that it can avoid many moral and certainly some mental disasters.

Do not be afraid to anticipate their curiosity; the real danger is that you may be late. Sexual education must always be in the nature of prevention not cure, prophylaxis not treatment. The worst thing of all is to arrive a day late.

Give them that education in the home, in the presence of God; at a time of day when they can go and play afterwards. Have a chat with each one individually. It will all come out naturally if it takes the form of just one more confidential discussion between you and them.

The father cannot avoid the responsibility by saying that it is the mother's concern, nor can the mother leave it all to the father. It is the responsibility of both. 'It will then be your duty to your daughters, the father's duty to your sons, carefully and delicately to unveil the truth as far as it appears necessary, to give a prudent, true and Christian answer to those questions, and set their minds at rest. If imparted by the lips of Christian parents, at the proper time, in the proper measure, and with the proper precautions, the revelation of the mysterious and marvellous laws of life will be received by them with reverence and gratitude, and will enlighten their minds with far less danger than if they learned it haphazard' (Pius XII).

What a wonderful opportunity you have to speak to your children about holy purity. Inspire in them love and enthusiasm for purity, in the positive sense, of mind, of eye, of lips, and of heart. Do not speak about impurity. A negative never has sufficient vigour to become an ideal.

Tell them how holy purity will give them the strength and courage of John when he remained, untarnished, at the foot of the Cross.

Tell them how it will give them the love of John, the young man, who could lean his head on Jesus' breast.

Tell them how it will give them the supernatural outlook of John, the apostle, who was the first to recognise the Lord walking on the water.

Speak to them of holy purity and of love.

Speak to them of the greatness of virginity, of chastity lived for love of God.

Speak to them of life lived in the light of love.

Speak to them of marriage and children.

Speak to them of the love between a man and a woman.

Speak to them of the greatness of the act of love.

Speak to them of how important it is to preserve for love their faculties of loving.

Speak to them of the divine character, here on earth, of human love.

If you are conscious of your mission, you will find and take advantage of thousands of opportunities that arise in the normal course of events to speak to your children – as well as about their books, hobbies, music and sport – of God, of life, of death and of love.

A FOOLISH MOTHER SPEAKS

'My child is an angel, he is really marvellous; sometimes he answers me back, but at his age the little fellow doesn't understand what he is saying. I don't mean he hasn't his faults; of course, every child has some defects, but somehow I find he is different from the others. He is so cute, and I am not saying that because I am his mother, I assure you. Just imagine, the other day he got two big chocolates, and straight away he said: "I'll give this one to Mary" – Mary is my little girl, you know. Really he is wonderful.

'No, his school report was not good this term. He is a very intelligent child, but he gets so distracted. Of course all children are like that. Now he is arranging his little office. It will be beautiful: he will have his table, his armchair, his own photographs, all nice and comfortable . .
.

'I'm sure he would love to go to Mass, but I couldn't allow it. It is so early in the morning, he might catch a cold. If the school began a little later I would like him to go, but at that hour of the morning . . . He is coughing like anything now, the poor child . . .

'But the poor child is only twelve, he is just a baby. I think so, but he has never said anything, and every year he writes his letter asking for the presents he wants. Last year, you know what he asked for? – Well, presents for Me! All I can say is . . .

'Certainly not; I wouldn't even mention those subjects. He is so innocent, the poor child. If you only knew him! It would open his eyes before the time! No, on no account. Yes, I agree, now that we are on the subject: I must say we have to be very careful with those magazines for children. Yesterday I had to take one of them from him. It was quite indecent, dreadful pictures! Of course the child understands none of those things, I am quite sure, but I prefer him not to have them. I found him also with some photos that I didn't like but . . . of course if he is collecting sportsmen . . . Anyway, I just don't understand the children of today.'

Now it is time for me to speak; I have tolerated enough of this nonsense. Mothers, those are the things you must not say. Try to realise that your children have grown up. Remember they are now at school they are learning many things.

A foolish mother's naïvety is paid for dearly.

And you, father, must not be naïve either. At least open your eyes and take some interest in knowing what your children are like and what they are doing. Don't tell me they are 'little darlings', because they are not! Children with big blue eyes and 'innocent remarks' can be villains.

Believe me, parents, I am speaking to you quite sincerely. You must show concern for your children. You think it is enough to pray for them, but you are wrong. The Lord wants you to form them, and discreet supervision is an essential part of that formation.

I am not trying to worry you. All I want is that you should show some concern for what concerns you. So I must tell you that your blindness worries me. The children of nowadays are just the same as you were, with the same passions as you, the same weaknesses, the same defects, the same temptations. Pray for them, yes, but also keep your eyes open.

SPEAKING OF THE WAY

> *Speaking of the early Christians, Athenagoras says: 'One might find many amongst us, both men and women, who are growing old in virginity, their hope being to have greater fruition of God.'*

When you have spoken to your children of the origins of life and of death, then remember to give them doctrine concerning the way, the path, we have to follow from the day we are born and are given our talents until the hour of our death, when the Master will return and ask us for an account.

Do you fully realise how much we all – you, I, your children and everyone else – have to get done on this earth while we are following our way, hard at times, at other times easy, but always cheerful for those who live as children of God? I may have spoken to you about the way many times already but it is no harm to insist on it again, because this is the really important thing and the only transcendental thing we have to aim at in life. And this is the way: to fulfil the will of God.

'I have called you by your name', the Lord says. And he has called us from eternity.

If only we realise how much, how very much, Jesus loves each one of us! Have you never asked yourself how it is that saintly men manage to remain cheerful always, even when their heart is tortured by dishonour, calumny and slander? But if God loves them and they love God, what do the ups and downs of this world matter?

This is the way your children must follow: the fulfilment of God's will for them. This is the great secret of happiness here, among the drudgery, difficulties and darkness of this earthly life; and this is also the great secret of an immense happiness hereafter for all eternity.

Help your children to find the will of God. Pray for them and bring them close to the Light that they may see it. For the Light is living, bright, splendid, when we look at it constantly, with generous eyes. But unless they are brought up to be generous then they will have great difficulty in seeing the path clearly.

We may divide the paths your children may take in life into two: either yours or mine, either marriage or full consecration to God. Pray very much that they may see what their vocation is, and that they may carry it out. It would be dangerous if your own mind were not clear on this question, because you will have to speak to them about the choice of their particular way. And there

162 • *God And Children*

is a lot of false doctrine going about, naturalistic and rotten, which is completely opposed to God's plan.

I have said many things about the sacrament of matrimony, and every word I said is true; the way of matrimony must lead to sanctity. But you must not think it is superior to consecration to God. The doctrine preached by Christ and by Saint Paul is that the excellence and advantages of full consecration of body and soul to the Lord are far above those of matrimony.

Be careful not to teach anything contrary to this doctrine, because 'it is solemnly defined as a dogma of divine faith . . . and explained in the same sense by all the holy Fathers and Doctors of the Church' (Pius XII, *Sacra Virginitas*). Surely by now you must have come to understand the point in *The Way* which says: 'Marriage is for the rank and file and not for the leaders of Christ's army'. But of course the rank and file can win the laurels.

You must not deform your children's consciences by suggesting that, because matrimony is a sacrament and virginity is not, the grace of the sacrament of matrimony makes that state more appropriate or more effective in uniting the soul with the Lord than dedication to God: 'All this is false and harmful doctrine' (Pius XII).

Be careful not to deceive them by saying that a father or mother of a family who publicly and in the sight of everyone professes to live a Christian life can produce greater spiritual fruit than they could if they dedicated themselves to God in the world or apart from it, because the Pope has condemned this idea in the Encyclical from which I have quoted.

Do not lie to them. And it is a lie to say that the Church of today is more in need of married men than of men dedicated to God, because the same text describes that attitude as 'most false and dangerous'.

You may have heard it said that young people have a vocation to marriage unless the contrary is proved, as if this were a presumption *iuris tantum*. This notion, which is so disturbingly common among parents, has emanated from people who are either very ignorant or not very truthful. And I am inclined to think that it is more ignorance than malice that makes them expound these erroneous ideas. I say 'erroneous' because that is what they are. They are theologically false and ascetically deplorable. If parents go on thinking like that, the time will come when there will be no priest left to bless the sacrament of matrimony.

Why do you try to give a tone of 'normality' to marriage as a vocation and of 'abnormality' to complete dedication to God? If the only standards you apply in these judgments are purely quantitative we would have to regard the saints as abnormal and indifferent, the selfish and the lazy as normal.

Taking the word normal to mean the norm, the rule, the means to an end, then in the supernatural field this (i.e. dedication to God) is the most normal vocation of all.

'What you must teach your children (and here I add not only children, but young people, men, fathers and mothers) is just this: that they have come into the world to glorify God, and that the only way that leads to happiness is the fulfilment of the divine will. They must therefore be given the means of knowing that will and they must be helped, by forming and strengthening them, to be generous in following it' (Cardona).

There are so many things you have to learn before you can teach your children and young people the way of life! So take the question of your own formation very seriously. If you ask me, I can give you a list of books to read: better, ask your own priest. You should not neglect this. However busy you are, you should give some time every day to reading. After all, how can you call yourself a Christian if you are ignorant of the things of God?

Only a grave lack of formation can explain that attitude of indifference, if not actual opposition, which is so common when the question arises of a son or daughter's vocation to a life of complete consecration.

Lord, you see how those people who think they are Christians are so sad when you call their children to live a life of complete dedication to the apostolate in the world! As you know well, when they are being baptised all mothers offer you their children, but they are very quick to change their mind if you try to take them at their word! Like the people of Gerasa, they are happy to have you with them, but they ask you to leave once you throw their pigs into the water in order to save a man.

Good Father, you see so many approach you like the rich young man, to ask the way to reach eternal life. But when you tell them, they go away, because they do not want to be leaders of men.

And how many Christian parents there are – at least they have been baptised into the faith – who, if they could choose the most sublime vocation for one of their children, would offer you the idiot son! It seems that the descendants of Adam's firstborn son are all a pack of misers! It is these same parents who help their children to get a Christian education but then begin to be frightened once they see them becoming 'too generous'.

How it must hurt you, Lord – for it certainly hurts me – to cry from Bethlehem, from Nazareth, from Bethany, from Calvary, from the Tabernacle, from the Gospel: 'If any man will come after me . . .' and then to see how few of them follow you!

Your children should get advice from a prudent but generous priest before finally deciding to choose a life fully dedicated to God and the apostolate. You yourselves have the right, the right and the duty, to make sure that those youthful impulses to give themselves to God are not mere dreams or silly fancies. You should make sure that they are thinking along supernatural lines. I hardly think there is any need to insist on this point. You are too jealous of your children's love to let them go away from you without testing their vocation.

Be careful, however, not to obstruct the will of God by inventing useless and dangerous tests, or by trying to provoke unjustifiable delays for no good reason. Do not fight against the plans of God. Certainly you may win for the moment, but later you may be the losers, you and your children.

'All those who wish to serve the Lord, when they see a soul called to God, should act thus: not observe human prudence too closely' (Saint Teresa).

Be careful not to suffocate a vocation under the pretext of testing it. Although it is not punishable by human law, it is at least as criminal to kill a vocation as it is to procure an abortion.

I could cite so many cases of these tests, set by 'Christian' parents! And, believe me, in some of them the strongest of the prophets would have failed! You must get it into your head that you cannot oppose your children's vocation. And you must get it into your head also that your children are bound to obey God rather than you – if such a clash should unfortunately occur.

Remember, my friends, that unjustifiable opposition to their decision may call down on you severe punishment from heaven.

Some parents fight against a divine vocation by all kinds of arguments, 'they even have recourse to means which can imperil not only the vocation to a more perfect state, but also the very conscience and the eternal salvation of those souls they ought to hold so dear' (Pius XII, *Ad Catholici Sacerdotii*).

'I have known several girls who were well disposed to my words [in praise of virginity] but they were prevented from coming here by their mothers . . . If your daughters wanted to love a man, the law would allow them to choose the one they loved. If they may choose man, why not let them choose God?'[1] These words of Saint Ambrose, addressed sixteen centuries ago to the mothers of Milan, could be repeated to many mothers nowadays.

If you behave in this way, putting obstacles in the way of your children's vocation, then you will have to take the responsibility for all the good that God might have done through them in the world of souls, but could not do because of your attitude. I certainly would not like to be in your place when the Lord comes to ask you to render an account. He was very hard on the lazy servant who buried his talent in the ground and did not make it yield fruit – you remember, he cast him into hell; so what will he not do to you, who actually rob the talent of their vocation from your children so that they cannot yield fruit?

'Open their eyes, my God; make them understand the meaning of the love they are obliged to have for their children so that they may cease doing them so much harm, and so that they may have nothing to complain of before God at the last judgment, when, whether they like it or not, they will understand the value of each thing' (Saint Teresa).

Do not be selfish with God. Do not confuse a sense of parenthood with a right of ownership over your children. Do not confuse your terms: love is not despotism.

If you offered your children to God when they were babies, now that they want to go to him let them go with your blessing. Our world needs people entirely dedicated to God; and God wants such people in our world. He wants saints and apostles to awaken the sleeping, to remind the forgetful, to enliven the indifferent, to give doctrine to men of all walks of life, that they may all serve the Almighty as true children of God.

Pray, pray very much, for your children; train them in generosity; mortify yourselves for them; speak to them of God; speak to them of souls; speak to them of the world we have to conquer for Christ. Love them as God loves each one of us: generously and disinterestedly. Then wait . . . and, as an Italian saying goes, if they are roses they will bloom.

The Lord tells us, in the words of Pope John XXIII: 'Our paternal and encouraging praise goes to those families who know how to appreciate and respect the gift of a vocation within their bosom and consider themselves happy to give the Lord some of their children, if he calls them. Let those families know that they have awaiting them the sweetest satisfactions on this earth and, especially, a bright crown in heaven.'

And Saint Teresa says: 'I sometimes think of the thanks they will give her, when they find that they are enjoying the eternal joys and that their mother was the means thereof, and I consider the accidental joy she will have on seeing them; and how different those will be who, because their parents did not bring them up as children of God, find both themselves and their parents in hell.'

Just as sorrow is the touchstone of love (cf *The Way*, 439) so a generous response to their children's vocation is the touchstone, the test, of the supernatural outlook of parents.

You should not be surprised if God calls your children – just as he called the twelve apostles among their boats and nets, and at their tax-gatherer's desks – to sanctify themselves and carry out an apostolate in the world by means of their human profession or career, as is the meaning of the dedication of the members of Opus Dei and others who seek Christian perfection in the world.

Do not be surprised that God should sow these vocations in the world, because he wants to heal the world from the inside, from its very roots, by infusing into it the life he brought when he lived among us. We see this now every day with our own eyes: men and women, fully dedicated to God, in every sector of society, in every kind of human activity. Precisely nowadays, when the world is crying out that never since its beginning has it gone through such critical times, precisely now the Church finds in her hands this most providential force.

Do not be surprised that as your children read the Gospel they find the Lord calling them, because in the Gospel Christ has left his clear and well defined invitation to all people and to all generations: 'If thou hast a mind to be perfect . . . '

Nor should you be surprised that you yourselves, within your married state, should be invited by the Lord to seek perfection, because these are the wonderful things the Lord is doing in this age of ours.

The world needs children of God who will live their Christian vocation perfectly.

A vocation is the greatest grace God can give anyone on this earth. It is undoubtedly a gift from God, which he gives freely and mysteriously; but it is a gift, I can tell you with Saint Jerome, which is given to those who ask for it. It is a gift that is granted to those who want it. It is a gift that is granted to those who work to receive it.

And here is how it is obtained: He who seeks will find.

This is why it is so: He who asks will receive.

And I insist on this because: To him who knocks it will be opened.

Speak to them, parents, speak to them of their way. Do not be cowards. Why are you afraid to bring them near the Light? Surely you want them, your own children, to live happily? Surely you want them to have that hundredfold here on earth?

Listen then. Saint Teresa in her *Way of Perfection* says this: 'God does not give himself completely until we give ourselves completely . . . But if we stuff our palace with petty people and things of no value, how can the Lord fit in there with his court? Among so much confusion he would soon tire.'

Surely you want your children to be happy here and more than happy hereafter in the kingdom of heaven?

Listen then. The Founder of Opus Dei told me this, and I want to pass it on to you: 'There are three things that bring happiness on earth and merit reward in heaven: firm, virginal, cheerful and unquestioning fidelity to faith, to purity and to one's way or vocation.'

SPEAKING OF SOULS

> *A home or a school where the children are not trained in the idea that to be a Christian means to be an apostle – with a duty to do apostolate – is a failure as a home or a school.*

Whatever the way the Lord has laid down for your children, one thing clear and quite definite is that he wants them to be apostles. If we are not bringing up our young people with an apostolic sense, with a deep and constant concern for the apostolate, practising apostolic deeds, then it is clear that we ourselves do not understand what Christianity means.

In spite of all we have already said, are you still unconvinced that you have a duty to form and shape apostolic souls? If so, then I have failed too, because that was the only purpose I had in mind. Surely I told you at the beginning that the education, the formation, of your children consists in helping Christ to be born and to develop fully in them?

Yes, Christ in your children! This is the great thing in your mission: to make Christ live in your children! Your task will be done, and done perfectly, when they are set on the road to acquiring zeal for sanctity and apostolate.

You are quite wrong if you think I am exaggerating in this. Have you ever stopped to think what God has done and is doing in the world of souls? Have you tried to realise the great things he would do in us if only we put ourselves in his hands?

Lord Jesus, how is it that we still do not understand your Will? Good Master, why is it that your blood thickens and clots in the veins of heartless men?

Good Jesus, make us understand once and for all that we children have to be perfect as our heavenly Father is perfect!

And, God, the thing is that we have millions, many millions, of Christian homes on earth. Is there anything we could not do with these millions of Christian families if we got down to it? We could overrun the whole world, for it is our world!

Good God, so many millions of Christian homes!

Parents, we can expect no forgiveness if we fail to lay this world of ours at the feet of Christ!

Your guilt will be tremendous if your children, after living for twenty years in your home, have not learned that to be Christians, men of Christ, they must be apostles. And let it be clearly understood that when I speak of apostolate I do not mean simply organising card drives for the poor at Christmas or collecting money for the missions. You have to show concern for the souls of your neighbours.

Andrew called his brother Peter; Philip brought his friend Nathanael; the Samaritan woman called the people of her town; mothers called their sons; the four friends of Capharnaum carried the cripple into the presence of Christ. The majority of Jesus' relatives did not believe in him, and yet we find three of them apostles. They are the sons of Alphaeus: James, Simon, and Jude.

THE SILENCE OF SORROW

> *'The Lord knows what each one can suffer, and when he sees that someone is strong, he does not hesitate to carry out his will in him' (Saint Teresa).*

Now I am quiet. You asked me to be silent, and you are right. There are times when it is better to say nothing, for silence can be so much more expressive than words. Those big strong strokes with which I have been writing to you – perhaps a little loudly – now become just weak letters, barely perceptible. When we speak of sorrow we cannot shout; when we feel sorrow we speak in a low voice and write in small letters.

Now there is nothing you can say to your children. You kiss them, you embrace them . . . but you have said all there is to say. They understand you. For the first time they have come up against sorrow, real sorrow. Up to now they have cried, sometimes, because they could not have something they wanted or because they were physically unwell, but always for more or less selfish motives regarding themselves personally. But now they have come up against a new sorrow, that hurts and tortures them in a way they never imagined possible: the sorrow of seeing that mother, whom they loved more than anything else in the world, lying dead.

You have poured out your soul, and walked away. The heart has two safety valves, two outlets, when it is overflowing with sorrow: the mouth and the eyes, speech and tears. And you have spoken little but cried much.

'Why should this happen?'

These were the few words you said, and you repeated them again and again for they expressed the whole intense tragedy going on inside you. Your children were there from the eldest, fourteen, to the youngest, four. The older ones were silent, while the youngsters ran about innocently and joyfully making noise. Your wife was there too, their mother, over there, asleep, deeply asleep, in a deep sleep of the body from which she will not awaken until the centuries have ended.

And again the same heart-rending cry: 'Why . . .?'

I was going to reply with a loud cry also, but I lowered my voice and, without looking at you, said quietly: 'I don't know'.

Neither of us could understand it. So we were silent. That was all we had to say. I looked up at the sky, a grey sky in which I could read only silence. Your eyes filled with tears.

'Why . . .?' And this time you made a sign to me to look at the children. Yes, it all seemed a great failure.

Amid the deafening noise from the traffic outside the window I could hear the sobs and the *Our Fathers*: Thy will be done on earth, as it is in heaven. It was the only consolation in that tremendous sorrow.

Now I can correct what I said to you before. The heart has in fact three outlets when it is overflowing with sorrow: speech, tears and . . . prayer. Thy will be done on earth, as it is in heaven!

Never before has my heart been so full of sorrow as it is today. I too want to unburden myself to someone now. Answer me this: which is sadder, the separation of a mother who has died or that of a son who is alive but . . . separated from God?

Poor mother, there is no sorrow like yours, and your tears flowed freely in the confessional. 'I have done everything possible for my son, but it is no good.'

The tone of voice, the tears, the complaints, your sorrow, all sounded somehow familiar to me. And before you had finished speaking, I understood. Yes, there they were, the same complaint, the same tone of voice, the same tears. That was just how Christ wept over Jerusalem when it would not listen to his call.

If you have really done everything possible for your son, then continue praying to the Lord, the King of all kings, asking him to take pity on you and on your son.

Prayers, cries, tears, petitions and requests, like those poured out by the Chanaanite woman for her possessed daughter; by Martha for her dead brother; by Peter for his unfaithfulness; by the mothers in Bethlehem for their murdered sons; by Jairus for his daughter; by that father for his lunatic son; by the centurion for his servant. Pray, weep, ask and implore, like the lepers, that the Lord may take pity on you and on your son.

There are times in life when we are faced with events that break our heart, and there is absolutely nothing we can do but pray, pray and ask, pray and pray. – Holy Mary, Mother of God. Ask and pray. – Pray for us, sinners, now. Now, now. Now and at the hour of our death.

So pray, mother, pray and implore. Pray, father, pray. Pray with your children. Even when you are tired, keep on praying, imploring. Only prayer can remove the obstacles. God expects you to pray and to keep on praying. What you are looking for is what Monica obtained for her son.

It may be – we do not know – that God has decided to grant you what you ask if you pray with perseverance, as he did for the Chanaanite woman, for Bartimeus, for Jairus. Pray and pray, for God, our Father God, is always good. So keep on praying.

Mary, holy Mary, you who got the hour of the first miracle brought forward so as to avoid embarrassment to a bride and bridegroom at a table without wine, intercede now for this son who pays no attention, who does not obey, does not pray, does not weep, does not love.

Jesus, you who offered unasked to wipe away the tears of a widow whose only son had been taken from her by death, have pity now on this sorrow.

Like Jairus I beg of you: Come, Lord, for my daughter is dying. I implore you like the Chanaanite woman: Cure my daughter, Lord. I cry to you like the father of the lunatic: He is my only son, Jesus, and he is suffering very much.

And I know, Lord, that you gave his daughter back alive to Jairus; you cast out the devil that was in the woman's daughter; and you cured the possessed lunatic.

Do not abandon this poor mother in her sorrow. Let her not wait in vain for your help. You taught us how to pray, so make our prayer effective now: Our Father, who art in heaven.

Here on earth we are too near sorrow, too closely attached to it, to be able to appreciate the other aspect of suffering. We see only one side of it: the side that hurts us. Seen from the earth, sorrow has no bright side, it has only shadows and thorns.

If you try to escape sorrow by merely holding hands with it, your hands will be covered in blood and you will be left in darkness.

Nor is it sufficient to kiss it lightly, for you will thus avoid being hurt further but the darkness will be just as deep.

You must embrace your sorrow tightly before you can touch its other side, the side that is seen from heaven. Then you will be filled with light, a light which comes down from on high, which penetrates deep into the heart and fills it with joy.

I am writing to you now late at night, after a day full of tears. Once again the noise of lorries can be heard through the window and it mingled with deep sighs and *Our Fathers*. Once again I see in my imagination the same scene as before: the dead mother and the little children playing at the foot of her bed. It is too painful to be able to sleep. I cannot console you in this, but God can. So keep on praying. Even if unbelievers laugh at you, continue to cry out to the Lord, and wait for the jibes of the faithless to die away.

Even when the feeling of failure is strong in you, never complain of the way God treats you. Even if the power of your prayer does not change the sad event, and your daughter dies, or your son remains a prodigal and refuses to return, you must never blame God for your misfortune. You can complain and cry out to him, but never against him.

Even when we do not understand, even then we must give thanks to our God.

Christ has left to the Last Day the explanation of all these sad events we meet with on earth. That will be within a few centuries, and then we will all be united again, including your dead daughter and your prodigal son; and the whole of humanity will then sing the triumph of our Christ.

On the Last Day our eyes will be opened, and then we shall see the reasons for your sorrow, the reasons for your tears, the reasons for death, the reasons for heresies, the reasons for the Church's sorrows, the reasons for all profane things, the reasons why the Lord permits what we on earth call sad things.

Thus saith the Lord: Let thy voice cease from weeping and thy eyes from tears, for there is a reward for thy work . . . And there is hope for thy last end, saith the Lord; and the children shall return to their own borders' (Jeremias 31, 16-17).

---

[1] *De Virginibus*, §58 in *The Nun's Ideals*, trans. Shiel, Dublin 1963, p. 39.

9

MAKE THEM STRONG

FREEDOM, FREEDOM, FREEDOM!

This is our slogan, this must be our slogan, if we want to be children of God. Freedom: we must cry aloud for it, demand it at all costs. The Church needs freedom, citizens of every country need it, parents and children need it.

Why, then, have you given up this great slogan?

Saint Paul tells us: Christ has made us free that we may rejoice in our freedom. And this love offreedom has always been deeply rooted in Christianity. The first lover of freedom is our Father God; then we, his children, follow him in that love. So great is it, that we will always choose rebellion rather than slavery.

When you see so much injustice and consequently so much sorrow in the world do not blame God. This is the product of our liberty, the liberty he has granted us men. He wants free men, not slaves.

Are you going to stand by and let yourself be deprived of that freedom which Christ won for you with his blood? What do you think you mean when you say that man is made in the image and likeness of God? In fact, what we reflect of God is precisely his unrestricted and unsubjected freedom of decision! How then can we accept slavery?

And because we are free, we are responsible entirely for all our own acts and to a great extent also for the events that happen around us.

If you want to educate your children in a Christian way, then bring them up 'in libertate gloriae filiorum Dei', in the glorious freedom of the children of God. And again Paul teaches us: 'Ubi spiritus Dei, ibi libertas', where the spirit of God is, there is freedom.

Take a look for a moment at this world, which is to be the scene of your children's life: so many false doctrines, unsound tendencies, erroneous principles, mistaken ideas, serious errors, gross ignorance about God, about his Church . . . Yes, take a look at this world, where your children are going to live their life: bad example, weak wills, corrupted and deformed consciences, malice . . .

And it is for this very world in which we are now living that you have to prepare those children. If they grow up weak-willed, or feeble, or selfish, or spoiled, or tied to your apron strings, then they will be of no use in the world of today. For they cannot escape being citizens of a country, members of a society, workers of one kind or another engaged in a great human task.

Your children – and the sooner they reach this stage, the better – will have to take on themselves and feel an intimate concern for the problems and preoccupations of their time and of their country.

They will have to share in the work and worries of all other men. They must be deeply interested and closely concerned in doing something worthwhile for others. They must belong to that group of audacious men who tackle and solve in a Christian way the tremendous problems of our time.

Your children will have to be men with political opinions, men of principles and judgment, with a well-formed conscience as regards the social, economic and political questions of our time. And now is the time to prepare them!

You must form them so that they will become members of the minority that leads the majority, although of course if you want them to turn out mere faces in the crowd, then you need give them no special formation. But remember, parents, that these indifferent attitudes are absolutely out of the question for a Christian. I shall have more to say about this point later.

If you have any desire to make your children capable of doing something worthwhile and being someone in life, if you really want to make them responsible Christians, then whatever else you do, please train them and bring them up in holy and healthy freedom, in the fullest and most complete liberty as regards professional, social, economic and political matters, in complete freedom of spirit. A genuine education consists in helping your children to be free and independent, able to stand on their own feet: do not lose sight of this. Their formation consists precisely in getting them ready to go through life alone. And yet we meet so many doting mothers and fathers who try, by every possible means, to make themselves indispensable.

The better formed a child is, the more deeply rooted will he have in him the spirit and the virtue of responsibility. But make no mistake about this: there can be no complete responsibility without genuine freedom. This must always be your ambition: to form your children in freedom, so that they will learn to handle it easily and skilfully.

For instance, the jump from a boarding school, with a strict disciplinary system, straight into university or working life can be quite fatal. You must prepare your children for this change in their life. One group of children I knew who were coming up to their last school examination were positively frightened at the thought that within a few months they would have to leave home and go to the university. What type of formation was that, parents? Is this another phobia you have given them?

Are you frightened by this question of freedom? For if you are afraid that freedom may be abused by your children, then it is clear that you have not practised it properly with them. I can tell you, although it may surprise you, that young people will abuse freedom only if you have not taken the trouble to make them free!

'Each family reproduces or tends to reproduce, on a small scale, the same thing that happens in countries', writes Canon Leclercq. 'The rulers, at the start, deny freedom to their subjects, under the pretext that they will make bad use of it; and then, when they have done everything possible to ensure that the subjects cannot learn to use it properly, they find themselves nevertheless compelled to grant it to them, and then they are right when they say that, in fact, the people make bad use of their freedom.'

You have passed through the stage when you had to tame the little animals creeping around on all fours; the time has also passed when your children did things 'because they were told to'; and the years are also gone when they did things simply to please you. The time is coming now when they are going to declare themselves independent in action and opinion. Biologically and psychologically they are becoming mature and independent. You must ask yourself whether you have formed their conscience properly, so that they will always be able to choose freely what is best.

You must be especially careful, mothers, to ensure that your children never look on their religion as a compulsory task. In the words of Cardinal Mindszenty, 'It is necessary that the young person should experience the sensation produced by living with the freedom and the unrestricted splendour proper to the children of God. He should feel proud to be a Christian! And not because his parents are also Christians, but because his own most intimate convictions impel him to it.'

Your children should be trained in Christian freedom so that they will be able to react properly when alone and confronted with a pagan world. And I see no greater obstacle to this healthy and holy formation in freedom than an excessively possessive love on the part of parents. Through misunderstanding the love they must have for their children, they end up by making slaves of them.

Parents, some of you are nothing less than dictators! Do you think that education consists of making your children have the same ideas and opinions as you have on every unimportant detail?

I have found parents so dictatorial that they think it their duty to impose on their children their own opinions on political, social and other such matters. Remember you cannot dogmatise on anything that is in itself contingent, relative or a matter of opinion. You cannot have a 'one-opinion-only' attitude in your family; and unfortunately many families have that. And those people always become absurdly dogmatic and intolerant on the numerous matters that God has left to the free judgment and opinion of men.

Remember that the only restrictions on the political freedom of your children – as on yours and mine – are the faith of Christ and the moral teachings of his holy Church. And yet so many try to dictate and 'standardise' all their children's opinions even on such variable matters as politics!

This subject will give you an opportunity of teaching them to carry on a discussion without raising their voice. And do teach them how to discuss. Certainly my generation – I cannot say if the same applies to yours – got neither political nor social nor sexual formation, nor any training in how to carry on a discussion, nor any clear understanding of what we Christians are meant to achieve in the world. This is another good reason why you should make an effort to teach it to the generation coming after us.

Perhaps one of your children will have a definite political bent and decide to make a career of taking an active part in public life. Teach him to do his work without bitterness and without trickery, to act with nobility, honesty and loyalty. The work to be done by holders of public offices is most important, serving as it does the interests and rights of both God and men.

Even if none of your children chooses politics as a career, you must still make sure to give them all a good training in civics; you must teach them all early in life that Christians, just as other men, have certain civic rights and duties which they cannot shirk.

So, train them in freedom. Make sure they do not grow up with the mistaken idea that the Church is interested in specific political formulas or systems. See to it that they never entertain the utterly wrong idea that Catholics should unite in a kind of great political party to achieve greater temporal power. This is a deplorable error, and may have catastrophic results. It would be equivalent to identifying Catholicism with a particular political party, and this would mean imputing to the Church all the failures and mistakes to which human undertakings are liable. It would make the Church answerable for the individual conduct of Catholics. And this we cannot allow!

Omit the word 'catholic' when you express your own opinions.

'Flee from that doctrinal error according to which some people wish to identify religion with this or that political party, to the point of declaring, or virtually declaring, that their adversaries are not Christians' (Leo XIII).

'Among the diverse systems, the Church cannot become a partisan of one way rather than of another. Within the ambit of the universal value of the divine law, whose authority governs not only individuals but also nations, there is ample scope and freedom of movement for the various forms of political systems' (Pius XII).

The Church tells her children clearly that she does not commit herself to any particular scientific, social or political system.

And just as you should speak to your children about the error of thinking that the Church is interested in specific political formulas, you must speak to them also of that other error, which regards the Church as totally indifferent to these questions. For, although the Church does not favour one system rather than another, she does indicate certain limits and points that are incompatible with dogma or morals.

Never cease giving your children clear ideas on such an important matter as this. Now, it can happen occasionally that the circumstances in a particular country are such that the ecclesiastical hierarchy may select one solution from among the many possible ones in order to safeguard the rights of Christ and his Church at that particular moment. In such circumstances – always genuine cases of emergency – the welfare of the Church and country demand strict unity of action and opinion on the part of Catholics in the face of certain threatening problems; those are times when one's personal point of view must be left aside in the interests of others.

Apart from these extraordinary circumstances which may come about in a particular country at a crucial moment in its history, all Catholics have the fullest liberty to form their own opinions and ideas on all these questions. We are of age, and with a proper sense of responsibility we must interpret the words I, you and he.

Your children should understand the idea of freedom in such a way that it will cause them no surprise to see parents and children active in opposing political par-

ties. And it is for you to give them that Christian understanding of freedom.

If you are afraid that politics may be the cause of
scandal, discord or disunity in your home, then the fault
is yours; if you are afraid that your children may be
divided by politics to the extent of harbouring hatred,
then the fault is still yours, because it is a blatant sign
that you have failed to form them in freedom and in
love.

And if, in spite of everything I have said, you still go
against freedom, then that is your own lookout; you will
go on being a tyrant and enslaving your children, a proud
tyrant who tries to establish dogmas unknown to the
Church, a very narrow-minded man, completely devoid
of universal outlook.

And how happy you can be in your mind with regard
to your children's salvation if you have formed them in
the liberty and in the love proper to the children of God!

> *Yes, each time more alive,*
> *– more deep and more high –*
> *The roots more entwined*
> *and the wings more free.*
> *The freedom of well-rootedness.*
> *The safety of infinite flight.*
> (Juan Ramon Jimenez)[1]

FREEDOM OF SPIRIT

Never be afraid of freedom. But you have to understand
what it means, for it does not mean leaving your children to their own devices and neglecting their education.

Indeed, to train them in freedom requires a constant
and healthy concern for them. This is a subject that
should come up for discussion in your confidential chats
with them very often. Freedom, which is a gift from God,

is the capacity that all men have to choose the appropriate means for the attainment of their end, which is, and can be none other than, God himself.

Now, the children's understanding is not perfect. Therefore you will have to watch what they are doing in order to ensure that they do not choose something which may appear good but in fact may harm them in soul or body.

Repeat to them as often as necessary that good is the only object of true freedom. To choose what is evil is not freedom, but folly. Freedom tends to the perfection of man and, consequently, its object is what is true and what is good.

Show them how dearly Christ paid for men's freedom, how he paid for it with his precious blood. So they must 'not let this freedom give a foothold to corrupt nature' (Galatians 5, 13).

Freedom resides in the will which chooses. It is in the will acting according to the light received from the intelligence. It is very important that your children should have great clarity of ideas, so that they can make good use of their freedom. It is the intelligence which lights and shows the way, and it is the will which then adheres to that light.

The obstacles to true liberty, that is to say liberty of spirit, are, on the one hand, ignorance and, on the other, the passions, which cloud the intelligence and weaken the will.

When we consider the matter in the light of all we have just said, it is easy to understand that friend of mine who said: 'I don't mind my children being bad so much as being foolish.' If they are foolish, ignorant or naïve in their attitude to life, it is to a great extent your fault. Foolishness is paid for dearly.

WILL AND DECISION

'So many young people are educated in our boarding schools with the greatest care; they are instructed and taught for many years; and yet when they leave school and begin to come up against the realities of adult life, we are sadly disappointed in them.

'Pupils who at school were models of discipline and pious sentiments, observant and devout in their religious practices, often become failures; some abandon their pious practices, they are careless about Mass and the Sacraments and even neglect their Easter duty; other even lose the faith and become indifferent or unbelievers.

'We try to explain all this by the environment in which our young people find themselves . . . but this only brings us to another deeper question: Why do catholic youths, who have for so long been subjected to a religious education and have given such manifest signs of benefiting from it, succumb so rapidly and completely to the environment?

'We can explain it only by saying that it is due to a lack of firmness, a lack of nerve or a lack of character. Their school education has not ceased to provide their souls with religious and moral knowledge accompanied by countless pious excercises. But for one reason or another that teaching has never penetrated into the most intimate part of their spirit, and taken firm root. They have not got the religious and moral principles to inform their life in a lively or effective way. The school devotions, practised with regularity, at the sound of a bell, have not been converted into a habit. As soon as the pupils no longer hear the bell or walk in lines to the chapel, all of those religious practices gradually totter or even crumble all at once. Looking at the results, we begin to wonder whether this zeal to give education has been of any use at all to the world.

'. . . Such young people were frequently considered to be exemplary and edifying while they were at school. That circumstance induces us to think seriously . . . whether this is really the type of instruction and discipline that is needed to fortify young lay people.'

To these words of Fr Hull I would like to add that the spiritual formation of children is not in direct proportion to the number of hours they are forced to spend in the chapel.

It is good to get them to form habits of skill and elegance in carrying out external acts; but we must remember that there is something much more important than this, which is to form their will, to train them to make personal decisions.

With compulsory Mass and general Communions we may solve the problem of statistics – which in any case, thank God, should not worry us in the least – but not the problem of forming young people.

Your children will soon be face to face with life, and there will be no bounds to break, no gates, no fences, no walls; they will find a limitless liberty, governed only by the first commandment of God.

Around the age of fifteen – it would be quite unrealistic to try to make them fully responsible for instance at twelve – as your children begin to get a feeling of their own intimacy and a consciousness of their freedom they should begin to realise that no one will solve their problems for them; they should begin to realise that very soon they will have to decide on their mode of conduct in every sphere; they must be ready always to do what is right and just, and they must do it properly, without compromising, without giving way to pressure, without bargaining, without being afraid of what people may say, without debasing or lowering their dignity in any way.

I wonder if you have heard that story about Berryer, a famous lawyer of a hundred years ago; Chevrot tells it. In a case involving vast sums of money, this lawyer with rigorous integrity refused to defend a cause that he did not consider just. His refusal to allow himself be persuaded caused some surprise. Someone said to him: 'You had only to stoop down and pick up millions.' 'Yes', he answered, 'but it would have meant stooping.'

Do not be afraid to foster that kind of holy pride in your children. 'Humility and the acceptance of divine aid', said Pope Pius XII, 'are quite compatible with personal dignity, with self-assurance and with heroism.'

'The numbers of qualities which our educational methods leave undeveloped, because they are not even thought of, is quite frightening. Undoubtedly if we were better informed, we would be scandalised less often by the surprises that the successes of adult life bring to the pessimistic future we had forecast for children whom we did not know well' (Le Gall).

'Lack of self-esteem and of a healthy respect for oneself', says Kieffer, 'shatters . . . the impulses of the soul, kills the spirit of initiative, creates passive and inert beings.'

Help them to have confidence in themselves, not to be presumptuous of course, but to be rationally confident. Do not hesitate to praise them for their abilities – for everyone has some – and the progress they make; for they need every support from their good friends, their parents. Show them the talents and potentialities that God has placed in their soul, and you will be amazed at the results.

It is not enough to encourage them to be audacious, to be men of enterprise and initiative. It is not enough to make them dislike the conduct of the insincere, the ignoble, the liars, the unjust, the cowards. You will never strengthen the will-power of young people simply by speaking to them of their duty, of loving their parents or of obedience to their superiors. It is not enough to train them merely by means of rules, regulations and routine. You must form their head and their heart properly.

You must teach them the theoretical principles that should govern their human actions. They should have a clear idea early in life about what they are trying to do, what they want to achieve, what they genuinely want to accomplish, because wanting is just useless wishful thinking unless it is wanting with their whole soul.

Give them opportunities to see for themselves how much a man can accomplish if he is willing to collaborate in everything with the energy that God gives through his grace.

Teach them to rectify their intention, to offer to God the tasks of every day without in any way lessening the human ambition they put into them, to channel everything human towards its proper and essential end.

Give them opportunities to exercise the faculty of making decisions. In the children's 'wanting to want', your help should be confined to suggesting solutions, but should never replace their own free and personal decisions. But do create situations in which they will simply have to make decisions one way or the other.

And when they have freely considered the situation make them carry out their decision immediately and efficiently, and forbid all useless reconsideration of the matter.

'I should not like you', says Saint Teresa to her daughters, 'to be women in anything, or even to appear to be women, but rather strong men; for if women do what is in them, the Lord will make them so manly they will frighten men.'

I would like you and your children to get this straight: good intentions are not enough when so many things can be accomplished with just a little more courage and effort.

SPOILING YOUR CHILDREN

> *'A son ill-taught is the confusion of the father' (Ecclesiasticus 22, 3). 'The child that is left to his own will bringeth his mother to shame' (Proverbs 29, 15).*

Parents, the time is approaching when you will find yourselves separated from your children. And if this thought makes you sad, it is because of what you may think is love but is in fact selfishness.

If you bring them up for yourselves then you are wasting your time; you will lose them anyway and very possibly you will spoil them, because you will bring them up badly.

It is not a question of 'allowing' your children certain, or even very many, liberties. The matter is much deeper than that. Fundamentally it means that they should live the sense, the feeling of freedom.

Only men who have learned self-control can be free. If young people are slaves of their own whims, it is impossible for them to have a sense of freedom. Freedom frees us, above all, from this very type of slavery.

Freedom is opposed both to over-strictness on the part of parents and to that over-indulgence which enslaves the children. Many mothers love their children with a love composed only of sweetness, a kind of sugary tenderness. But true and genuine love desires only the good of the beloved, so it is composed of sympathy with severity, patience with intransigence, understanding with firmness.

Spoiling your children is not love, it is frivolity. In love you give yourself, in spoiling them you seek yourself.

To spoil or pamper them: that is one of the great dangers. It sometimes happens that parents who themselves had to fight hard for success in life, who had to overcome great obstacles and innumerable barriers, who had to suffer heavy blows and hard knocks from friends and enemies, try, when the time comes, to make life easier for their children. And this is a grave mistake which is paid for dearly in this world.

And other parents, who were brought up too strictly, run the same risk, because they remember the hardship they themselves suffered from their own parents, and they try to make life too soft for their children. They load them with comforts; they protect them from any kind of unpleasantness or difficulty; if they could – weak mothers! – they would suffer in their place; they pamper them outrageously and weaken their will; they give in to all their whims. They think they are protecting them, but in fact they are denying them the slightest chance of acquiring experience . . . Well, it is their own lookout!

A normal child, who might turn out to be someone great in life, may grow up to be completely useless because of being spoiled, petted, pampered, flattered, kissed and hugged at all times.

If your children do not learn to control themselves now in the hard struggle of puberty, later on you will find they have grown into useless puppets, without strength, with no mind of their own, at the mercy of every wind, going from one fall to another, from one failure to another. And then neither money, nor the family name, nor their social position, nor even their talent will be strong enough to drown the voice of conscience: Was it for this that you brought them into the world?

Do not try to insure an easy life for your children; you must make them tough so that they can confidently face a hard life. Get them used to making an effort. Get them used more to wanting than to wishing.

'If man had not had to fight against the world', says Chevrot, 'he would still be living in caves.'

Your children's life will be a great one if, when they meet with adversity or difficulty, they make an effort, struggle, deny themselves, overcome and triumph.

If you want to make them free make them strong.

When you see them suffer you should not become soft. You should not tell them lies when you have to take them to the doctor; do not hesitate to demand effort on their part; have confidence in their strength and courage. Stimulate that heroism which lies hidden in every child's soul.

Boys do not cry at the sting of disinfectant on a cut when they are at school, but at home the tears flow when a loving mother puts it on saying: 'Poor child, you must be in terrible pain.'

You want to bring them up in a manly way? Well, take note.

A fixed hour for getting up.

A fixed hour for going to bed.

More cold showers than warm baths.

Unless the child is sick, he must eat normally whatever is put in front of him.

A temperature of 98.4 shows that they are fit to go to school.

They should not ask anyone to do things for them which they can do themselves.

Means of transport to school are: feet, bicycle or public transport, but never get out the car just because they are going to be late.

Teach them to finish everything fully and properly. This is a difficult art to practise, possibly one of the most difficult of all.

Get them to swim, someplace where they will not need a lifesaver to pull them out, but do get them to swim (this is a bit out of context here, but I had to say it somewhere).

Pray to the Holy Ghost to give your children the gift of fortitude; it will add to the human strength which they themselves have achieved by repeated effort, a cheerfulness and ease in which the divine aid will be evident.

But if you want to give your children an upbringing that will fit in perfectly with their own whims, then let me quote you these lines which were actually written in earnest, although they sound like a joke: 'We consider', says the Director of a new school, 'that the horn is the most appropriate instrument to awaken the child. His awakening begins with a reveille which is almost inaudible, as if the instrument were scarcely being blown; little by little the intensity of the notes is increased; then they are repeated and repeated, and the children thus awakened hear the same music at the end of their sleep as at the beginning of their awakening. With no commotion, no alarm, no shrillness, life awakens in the school as the sun rises on the horizon . . . '

If you like to amuse yourself with this new method, then by all means buy a hunting horn; but if what you want is to get the child out of bed, then prod him with it. Getting up will always be unpleasant.

Children must be taken seriously; they are not toys for the parents to play with. But neither can they be toys for themselves. Every child has within himself a little king, a king who must be neither smothered nor enslaved; a king educated in freedom who should place himself at the service of others. If the child is spoiled and satisfied in his every whim, then the little king inside him becomes the protagonist, the most important character, the centre of the family world: and this is another dangerous mistake that should be avoided at all costs.

Now that your children are becoming fond of reading, give them a present of *The Way* and let them open it at point no. 295: 'If you are not master of yourself – though you may be powerful – your air of mastery moves me to pity and laughter.'

Freedom. Self-mastery. Self-control. Discipline. Willpower. If what you want is to make of your children men

194 • *God And Children*

and women with a sense of responsibility, then you must realise that they need a lot of freedom, ability to consider a problem, ability to make a decision and a strong will to put it into practice.

HUMAN VIRTUES

> *'They must give good proof of utter fidelity': This is the advice that Saint Paul gives to Titus, to servants and to children.*

You ask me what I think your children should be like?

Well, I would like them to be loyal, sincere, hardworking, generous, courageous, straightforward, broadminded, determined, decisive, tenacious, always cheerful, lively, strong-willed, with many human virtues directly or indirectly rooted in the cardinal virtues, complete and 'whole', in the fullest sense of the word, in their conduct and actions, faithful in doing their work, and apostles in their professional sphere.

What joy it gives me to see parents busily training their children in sociability, sensitivity, good taste, elegance, refinement in dealing with people, good manners and civic spirit.

And it makes me sad to think of the parents of those children whom I see destroying everything they find before them in the countryside. Have those parents not taught them why God made the flowers?

Every one of your children's natural abilities and faculties must be developed. And you must help them to perfect those faculties by integrating them with their supernatural life, their interior life: in that way their human life will be ennobled. They will then have a more effective basis, not only for the spiritual and eternal order, but also for the material and temporal.

We have agreed, I think, that we want to make of your children truly Christian men and women. But no one can be a true Christian unless he tries with all his strength to be a saint and an apostle.

Let us now read something on the question of human formation.[2]

'There are two motives which should impel one to acquire the moral virtues: the first because this acquiring is part of the ascetical struggle normally necessary in order to achieve perfection; the second, because it is a means to exercise the apostolate more effectively.

'As regards the first of these motives, let us remember that the moral or natural virtues are, as it were, necessary and pre-requisite elements, raw material, energies which can be harnessed and made much more productive.

'. . . In the ascetical struggle, the development of the natural energies obviously precedes, in the logical order, that of the supernatural virtues; but in the practical order, the two developments are concomitant and go hand in hand. Thus, the natural virtues are an integral or potential part of one or other of the four cardinal virtues, which for any man are a consequence of the right use of his reason, and which Christians receive raised to a supernatural plane by grace in Baptism. We deduce therefore that the natural virtues are not only a means for the ascetical struggle, for exercising the supernatural virtues, but that they are also, for the soul in grace, a consequence of charity.

'Thus we understand why the Church should demand of her saints the heroic exercise, not only of the theological virtues, but also of the moral or human virtues, and why people who are truly united to God by the exercise of the theological virtues become perfect also from the human point of view: they become refined in their dealings with people, they are loyal, affable, courteous, generous, sincere, precisely because all the affections of their soul are placed in God.

'. . . At the end of the ascetical struggle, when one lives united to God, it is possible to live the human virtues supernaturally: with simplicity, day by day, and with supernatural naturalness.

'. . . If, as has already been said, the exercise of the natural virtues – as a part of human formation – is necessary in order to achieve perfection, to reach sanctity . . . we must now note that their exercise is also necessary as a weapon of apostolate: more concretely, for the apostolate of example. It suffices to quote in this respect the enlightening words of Pius XII: "If it is true – as undoubtedly it is – that supernatural grace perfects and does not destroy nature, the edifice of evangelical perfection must be founded on the same natural virtues. Before a young man becomes an exemplary religious, he must try to become a perfect man in the ordinary things of every day: he cannot climb to the heights of the mountain if he is unable to walk securely on the plain. Let him learn, then, and show in his conduct the dignity proper to human nature: let him dispose his person and his presence with decorum, let him be faithful and truthful, keep his promises, control his words and actions, show respect for everyone, not encroach on the rights of others, be patient, amiable and, what is more important, obey the laws of God. As you well know, possession of and formation in the supernatural virtues disposes a supernatural dignity of life, especially when someone practises and cultivates them in order to be a good Christian and a proper herald and minister of Christ".'

What is there for me to add to these words?

Just make sure you do not disrupt, but rather stimulate and supernaturalise, all those human virtues in yourself and in your children; make sure you introduce them at the right time into the world of human relations, because there are many, very many, indeed countless, young people who fail, not so much for lack of knowl-edge, as for lack of that elementary wisdom that is called 'getting on well with people'.

HONESTY

> *'Even unto death fight for justice, and God will overthrow thy enemies for thee' (Ecclesiasticus 4, 33).*

So your children tell lies? Well, examine yourselves slowly and carefully, and take the blame on yourselves; if you correct yourselves they will be corrected.

If they lie, usually it is in self-defence or as a shield against the cane. For the child who trusts his parents and his teachers fully does not lie. Children tell lies when there is an atmosphere of mistrust in the home. But they were born sincere, and, most of the time, they lie because they are afraid of you. So: correct yourselves and they will be corrected.

Or perhaps they lie because they are imitating you – an even better reason why you should correct yourselves.

Never test your children to see if they tell lies. This is a fault which parents often fall into. If you know that a child has done something wrong, let him see clearly that you know it, but never pretend not to know and ask him if it was he who caused the trouble. Never put your chil-dren in a situation where they will be tempted to lie; speak out before they have a chance to tell the lie. And never accuse them in front of strangers of telling lies; such a humiliation would be too severe and they would lose their confidence in you.

There is a school I know that has a shield covered with hearts and crosses, and the motto on that shield is: 'Let our yes be yes, and our no be no'. This could also be the motto of your home. In that school loyalty, faith-ful fulfilment of the laws of fidelity, honour and honesty, govern the pupils' relations with God, their teachers, their companions and themselves.

We learn truthfulness and honesty by seeing truthfulness and honesty practised around us. For instance, when you draw lots among your children do not write numbers on bits of paper so that they can all be sure afterwards that you did not cheat. Just think of the number and give the prize to whoever guesses it. Believe me – and I am not lying now in telling you this – in these eight years I have been living among schoolboys, there has never been one who thought of saying that I had cheated and given the prize to someone who had not guessed the correct number.

The right atmosphere can be so effective! And I assure you that you too can create that climate of truthfulness and honesty in the home if you yourselves love and practise that virtue.

HARD WORK

> *'If he has no craft provide for him according to your understanding, so that no man shall live among you in idleness because he is a Christian. But if he will not do so, he is making traffic with Christ; beware of such people'* (The Didache)[3]

We men are made to work. It is something we cannot avoid, under pain of shirking the duty imposed on us by God. Hard work is the ordinary way of sanctification for parents and children; habitual idleness does not lead to sanctity.

We must work hard and well, and this for two reasons: the good of the community and the good of the individual.

You and your children should approach the tasks of life with this holy idea: that man must do things more and more perfectly, thus contributing to human progress, and that at the same time he must himself become perfect by means of his work, thus fulfilling the divine plan concerning things and men.

'The unfortunate thing about the contemporary world is that while lifeless matter emerges ennobled from the workshop the person becomes debased in it and loses his value' (Pius XI).

If work is done seriously, honestly, conscientiously and in an orderly way, it sanctifies the worker. But reluctance, hesitation, laziness, procrastination, discouragement and delay are stumbling blocks on the road to sanctity through work.

Teach your children to finish things fully and properly. Far too many people leave the sign 'Temporary surface' for ever and ever on the road behind them.

The expression 'I've done enough' is the very antithesis of perfection, for 'I've done enough' is, by definition, equivalent to leaving things unfinished. It is contrary to the spirit of Christ, who 'did all things well' (Mark 7, 37). It is the blight that destroys many a crop of good deeds.

The human aspect of our ordinary things must be done perfectly, so that they may be acceptable from the divine point of view. If we do things by halves we shall never become saints.

We say 'I've done enough' when we are working against our will. So it is very important to put human ambition and enthusiasm into the work we are doing. Human ambition and enthusiasm are the first step toward perfection, and human perfection is the bridge to divine perfection.

Get your child really interested in the things you want him to learn.

'I've done enough' and 'It's useless' are two wrong extremes. Be on the side of perfection.

Now we come to the question of the children's studies. The great worry of parents nowadays is this: 'I hope he passes'. All their great ambitions centre around that point. Poor parents!

The first disillusionment I had as a teacher was when I met a mother who told me: 'I like all that human and supernatural education they try to give my son, but the only thing I am really interested in is that he get his exams.'

This is one of the deplorable results of lack of formation in parents. Results, marks, reports and, above all, examinations are things on which the whole family honour is thought to depend. Surely you see that it is all wrong to make a tragedy of your children's little academic failures? For them, examinations are as if they were on trial for their life!

The parents want the child to study so as to uphold their honour, and the child studies just so as to pass. Surely there is something wrong in all this?

Even among teachers, although they are the exceptions, we find some who boast of the great number of examinees they fail in the annual examinations. They do not seem to realise that for a teacher who spends the day with his pupils and whose duty it is to teach them, a failure of theirs is a failure on his own part, two failures are two failures on his part and many failures are many failures of his.

Let us stop and think for a moment about what exactly we want to accomplish with our children's studies.

In the literature class – I suppose the same thing happened to you – we were taught a little about each famous writer: a bit about his life, where he was born, whether he got married, whether he was acclaimed during his lifetime and whether he fell down the stairs just before he died, and lots of titles of books, so that we could say them off quickly when we were asked about him in the examination. All so marvellous and astounding!

If we wanted to get a distinction we had to know a summary of several of his works which, naturally, we never read. And everyone was so happy about the whole thing! (The other system, of taking up a little work and dissecting it into tiny pieces and forgetting to ask who wrote it or who or when he was is just as bad . . .)

Look: along with the syllabuses of subjects they have to study for their examinations, concentrate on these four things, which are the most important things for the first sixteen years of your children's life as students: they should learn to read; they should learn to speak; they should learn to write; they should learn to study, in two languages. Then in the second sixteen years of their life they will be able to read, speak, write and study on their own, alone, without supervision, without threats of punishment, without private tutors. You cannot spend your money on such useless and even harmful luxuries!

If you want to insure their future, get them used to making an effort.

If a child who goes to an ordinary school or college needs a private teacher or extra classes in order to pass his school certificate examinations, it is possible that he should give up studying! There are thousands of better ways of wasting his time! If he knows that when he gets home there will be someone to repeat what he was told in class as many times as necessary for him to learn it, then naturally he will pay little attention in class.

It is those same students who had private teachers while they were at school who, when they go to university, ask if they must learn the footnotes also!

Parents, be humble enough to ask the teachers how much you can expect of your children. Your collaboration in this way is necessary for their good.

As to the best and most effective means of getting them to study, just remember that it is as disastrous to be weak and spoil them by giving in to every request as it is to be absolutely inflexible and never give in.

You and the teachers should agree on a target for each child. And never compare one with another, whether his brothers, his cousins or any other children, for they have nothing to do with his individual case.

Among your children there may be some who are sensitive or excitable, for whom severity – if we are to believe the educationalists – would be inadvisable and would only have undesirable effects. But on the other hand it is good to be very strict with those amorphous types who should be allowed no possibility of escape. The way to treat these amorphous types is to get them into a corner: 'On the one hand they should be shown the effort that is expected of them and the practical or moral rewards that will be theirs if they make that effort; and on the other hand they should be told the penalty or sanction. Their objective sense will decide them to take the right direction' (Le Gall). A boarding school can be very beneficial for this type of boy. Anything rather than a doting mother who will spoil him.

As I said, never compare your children with others, for there can be no proper basis of comparison. Compare each one with himself.

And do not be naïve; never set yourselves up as an example for them, lest you provoke a scene like one I had to endure some time ago. It began with the school report, which was anything but favourable. There was only one good mark and that was for drawing; all the other subjects were very bad. The father was in very bad humour, and the child was in tears.

'At your age I was getting distinctions in these subjects. What have you to say for yourself? Speak up. Say something.'

And sure enough the boy spoke up: 'I'll tell my children exactly the same thing!'

A final point: do encourage your children to have some hobby or interest outside their studies. If they have no time for hobbies, it can only be because the study timetable is badly drawn up.

The studies of a boy who has no free time left over for reading, music, painting, some manual work or sports are as badly planned as is the work of a father who cannot find time to attend to his wife and children.

If the school which your children attend does not organise some clubs or societies to teach them a hobby which will amuse them later on in life and help them pass their free time, then it is up to you to do so. All work and no play . . .

[1] Translated by Douglas Mellor.

[2] Alvaro del Portillo: 'Formación humana del sacerdote' in *Nuestro Tiempo* No. 17, Pamplona.

[3] Trans. Kirsopp Lake, London 1930.

10

LET THEM GO

THE TIME HAS COME

I cannot finish this book without speaking to you, once again, of the world in which your children are to spend their lives.

The time has come when you have to let them make their own way in life, having strongly impressed on them something which is not just a word, but a way of life: responsibility.

With tears in your eyes, or at least in your heart, you will see them leave you and take the path that God has marked out for them from eternity. You will see them take that path confidently and without turning back. They are full of youth, full of that healthy optimism that permeates every truly Christian life.

You, parents, will always have that concern, that insecurity of not being quite sure whether you have really done all in your power to make them men, Christians, saints. And I cannot solve this problem for you. On the Last Day, when time ends for you all, when you finally leave your home and cross into a happy eternity, you will see clearly how much you have done and how much God had wanted you to do.

But have confidence; trust in your Father God who will continue to watch over your children. Have confidence in the powerful aid of the Angel who will accompany each one of them through all the ways of the earth. These were the words of the Archangel Raphael to Tobias who, like you, was blind and was worried about his son's departure: 'I will lead thy son safe'. And when your wife cries, as Anna, Tobias' wife, cried, as your own mother cried and as all the mothers in the world cry and ought to cry, tell her: 'Dry thy tears. Safe will he fare, this son of ours, and safe return; I hold it for truth that an angel of the Lord escorts him' (Tobias 5, 22-27).

But now . . . your child is getting ready to leave home; there is no time to waste, so I would like to tell him something I have not yet had time to tell you. So make up your mind: either you tell it to him or you leave it to me. But I would not like him to leave your house without hearing what I have to say.

Better still, the three of you could listen to what I have to say now. Call your wife and your son now, before he goes away with his Angel.

LOSING THE FAITH

> 'I let them go according to the desires of their heart'
> (Psalm 80).

Again and again we hear it said that the world is becoming unchristian. The atmosphere is becoming more and more pagan; institutions, homes, customs and nations are losing the faith.

These are sincere and sorrowful cries that come from hearts fully conscious of the weight of their responsibility. Sociologists and thinkers tell us that we are going through the greatest crisis that the world has yet known. Never before has there been such apostasy among all social classes. Theologians add that the sense of sin has disappeared.

For myself, I can only agree that the crisis affecting our world is really enormous and universal. It is not only we catholics who are suffering it; it is also affecting muslims, buddhists, protestants and brahmans. It is a crisis affecting the very idea of religion. Pope Paul VI, when still Archbishop of Milan, wrote a penetrating letter on this subject, which you would do well to read.[1]

But one thing there is not – because there cannot be – is a crisis in the Church of God. For Christ triumphed forever over sin, death, pain and Satan. What the Church is suffering – and it is only to be expected, since she is immersed and steeped in things human – are mere scratches and pinpricks, accidental changes. But have no fear. The Church will remain alive always: we have God's word for that.

I too have often wondered about the same question as you are asking yourself now. And the answer is this: the only important cause of all this chaos that mankind is undergoing at present is that we have all – all of us – taken miserable man himself and placed him at the centre of man's life. This is the cause of the world crisis. And the only solution is this: we must place God, once again, in his rightful place.

We have centred everything around ourselves. For centuries past, life has been revolving around 'me'. But if I am concerned with love, it is essential that 'I' tend away from 'me' and towards 'others'; these 'others' are God, whom we must love above all things; the world, for which we must have a great ambition: the ambition of improving it and making it Christian; and other men, for whose benefit we have received a vocation for service.

This diabolical centering of everything around man is the cause of our constant forgetfulness of others. We have left God outside our life, outside our way. This is where we are to blame.

GOD'S INTERESTS IN OUR WORLD

> *'His reign, as we know, must continue until he has put all his enemies under his feet' (1 Corinthians, 15, 25).*

We must put God back on that high throne where men have seated themselves so comfortably. You have only to open your eyes wide and you will see the great ambitions – the ambitions and the interest – that God has in our poor world!

The first Christians carried out the program laid down for them; and with that love of God and of souls infused into them by the Lord himself, they transformed and christianised a whole pagan empire, by prayer and hard work at the very centre of that empire. But what is happening today? Today – indeed from the time of the Renaissance onwards and increasingly from the eighteenth century – the enemies of the Church have displaced us from society. We have allowed them to displace us through our lack of doctrine and courage – through lack of love of God. For we are ignorant of the interest that he has in our world.

Christ is absent – I am speaking now above all national frontiers – from the minds that govern our education, our press, our radio, our movies, our television, our industry and our labour, the world of finance, the world of public administration, the worlds of thought and action and organization, the worlds of art, of science, of politics. And he will continue to be absent unless we tell our children of the tactics used by the enemies of God to produce – because they have now successfully produced – an atmosphere and environment receptive to the satanic idea that religion is a private affair which must be relegated to the sphere of conscience. They want to confine Christianity to consciences! And our grandfathers accepted these errors!

Those people want to deform the true meaning of Christianity. They want to exterminate all Christian influence in society. They want to confine the Church to churches, and let it limit itself to baptising children and burying corpses. They want to limit the Church of Christ to worship and the administering of Sacraments, under the pretext that her dominion has its roots in the invisible world of souls. They want to eliminate all Christian activity in public life.

So, parents, be on the alert, because there are many ignorant – or bad – Christians who are playing into the hands of God's enemies. You cannot allow your children to leave home with these diabolical ideas that we have been accepting for centuries past.

So, Christianity is not a religion concerned solely with the relations between man and his Creator. The mission of Christianity is not to make those who are afraid of the earth look for comfort towards the kingdom of heaven.

The essential action of our Christianity certainly aims at maintaining and developing an intimate contact between humanity and God; it aims at bringing the soul of all men nearer to him; it aims at making us all live as children of God.

But Christianity is not only that; there is much more to it! It is not concerned exclusively with eternal life. It is not interested merely in the hereafter. It is also interested in what is here.

What do you think it should do? Leave the earth in the hands of Satan? Why have you still got this idea? Why are you so ignorant about what Christ wants of his Church? Why have you let his message be snatched from you? What do you mean when you say 'Thy will be done on earth, as it is in heaven'? Christ wants to reign in eternity and in time, in heaven and on earth.

We must restore all things, everything, in Christ. The whole of creation is anxiously 'waiting for the sons of

God to be made known' (cf Romans 8, 19). All things, 'all that is in heaven, all that is on earth', must be united under one single head: Christ (cf Ephesians 1, 10). Try to realise, once and for all, the meaning of these words: 'all that is in heaven, all that is on earth.' This comprises everything, absolutely everything: family, the state, economy, finance, philosophic doctrines, laws, institutions, every human profession, scientific research, artistic creation; man, life and death; peoples and nations – all must reflect the spirit of Christ.

I would like to quote you this enlightening passage written by a friend of mine: 'It is an unquestionable fact that man has been raised to the supernatural order, and this change embraces all the manifestations and all the activities of human nature, including its social aspects.

'It is erroneous to wish to confine the supernatural order to the "internal forum" of consciences and to exclude its effectiveness from the sphere of society and, therefore, of public opinion, which is an essentially social phenomenon.

'And this attitude, which at times affects the mode of actions of some Catholics, is far from the truth, because the common good of society is inseparable from the supernatural end laid down for us by God.

'When he redeemed the world by dying on the Cross, Jesus Christ drew all things to himself – "omnia traham ad meipsum" – so that nothing human, nothing relating to that nature which he assumed and which he saved, can remain in a sphere that is indifferent to the supernatural order.

'His redeeming sacrifice is effective for the whole of man's nature, including all his relations with God, with other men and with all creatures; therefore the salutary effect of the Redemption penetrates to the very roots of the social order.'

We must never forget, parents, that Christ cried to the world: 'I am Life', and he is the only Life. The individual with all his problems, the nations with all theirs, all human activities – in short, the whole of creation – are made for God and depend fundamentally and radically on him.

We must not forget that Christ cried to the world: 'I am a King'. Do you too laugh at this assertion of his, as did the Roman Governor who was so afraid of losing his post? Or are you one of those who misunderstand our Lord's words? Do you think when he said 'My kingdom does not belong to this world', he intended to leave the earth to the devil?

The kingdom of Christ is unlike the kingdom of this world, in that he received it from his Father God. We can distinguish two moments in this kingdom of God: the final or eschatological moment, the consummation, and the other moment here, the reign of Christ on earth, in the present world, in human history. There is one in eternity and another in time. It is this latter phase that wicked men want to deny us.

It is understandable that men without faith should be willing to leave us the kingdom of hereafter, because they do not believe in it and it does not concern them. What hurts them – as it hurts the devil – is that God should want to reign also in this temporal world; not only in the sacred sphere, but also in the profane. What they want is to confine religion to the interior sphere, thus smothering all the influence the faith may and should have on men's professional, civic, political and social activities. But this dissection of life, this break in the unity of the human person into stagnant compartments, is illogical and repulsive.

'I am a Christian', said Terence, 'and nothing that is divine or human is foreign to me.'

THIS IS YOUR MISSION

> '*The mission of the Church is not only to baptise all men, but to baptise the whole man and everything in the man. The Church wishes to penetrate into and win for Christ the whole of historical humanity. Because her outlook is catholic, it is universal, and there is nothing that can be foreign to it*' *(Cardinal Suhard).*

We must restore all things in Christ; 'not only,' as Saint Pius X says, 'that which belongs directly to the divine charge of the Church, which is to win souls for God, but also everything which derives from that charge, which is Christian civilisation in the aggregate of all and every one of the elements which constitute it.'

But when you think of this great task which the Church – Christ prolonged – has to fulfil, do not for a moment imagine that it is the priests, religious and nuns who have to intervene in the world of profane things, thus giving them a blacker tone. This frightening type of 'clericalism' would be dangerous, erroneous, false and quite useless. It is not the business of us priests to run temporal things; these secular functions are out of the question for us. Our work is to bring your souls nearer to God and nourish your interior life so that it will overflow into apostolic yearnings.

It is for you, parents, to play an active part in these worldly matters. You – and remember you are the Church – have this wide field of apostolate as a duty of your state in life. On your shoulders lies the responsibility for the apostolic progress of human society. It is for you, lay people, to carry out this immense task, encouraged and aided by those souls dedicated to God in undertakings such as Opus Dei, who by divine vocation live in the world of profane things, submerged in God and in time, sanctifying their ordinary work, to which, under pain of straying from the search for perfection, they are devoted. Since they are lay people in the world like you they have the same field of action as you and, because they give themselves entirely to God, they have a spirit which you can bring to your own thought and action.

Such are the great things that God has done in this age of ours! They are a kind of push from the Holy Ghost to us Christians to make us work zealously and tirelessly for the reign of Christ on earth.

You who have been called by God to serve him in the middle of the world, and not in the cloister or in solitude, have to live with many human worries and cares, side by side with other men, each one carrying out his particular task. So you are concerned in a direct and very special way with all the problems, all the circumstances and all the events of social life. And this is your mission which carries with it a grave responsibility: the responsibility of co-operating with Christ to give the world the direction he wants to give it.

What are you doing there looking foolishly about you, so distracted? Why are you standing there idle? Has no man hired you? Come with us, then. If no group of men has offered you a clear and brave plan to fill the world with courage, then come with us. Come, you and your children. There is plenty of work to be done, work for many, work for all. We want to give the world the features the first Christians wanted to imprint on it. We must continue the work they began.

The blood that flows in the veins of the world is corrupted; it needs a transfusion which only Christians with hearts of kings can give it. Only children of God who are willing to let their flesh and muscle be torn to shreds can produce that life-giving change.

In this evolution of our world you, mothers, have an important role to play. You must not believe anyone who tries to offend you by saying the transformation will be brought about entirely by men. In fact you have always been the best collaborators in the Church's apostolate.

It was you, strong women, who were left at the foot of the Cross, just you and a young man, John. It was you, daring women, who, defying every human law, went to the tomb at that difficult time when the men had closed the doors of the house for fear of the Jews. And Christ rewarded you by making you apostles of apostles.

Supernatural prudence will always point the way, but it will be courage and daring that will make us follow it.

You have now in your strong and capable hands thousands of young children who will go out into the world tomorrow as you have formed them today. So you must realise that this is your great, your really great, mission.

In the first place, form yourselves. You cannot hope to give doctrine unless you first have it, unless you are formed. Do you honestly think that God will make up for your laziness? Your own formation, then, and the education of your children! Bring them up with this aim in mind: that they may be Christians deeply concerned with everything that is supernatural and eternal in their soul and everything that is temporal and profane in the world.

Teach them the spirit of faith, that they may have the daring to win back those godless souls for Christ.

We are responsible, you and I and your children, just as all Christians are responsible, for that gift we have received from our Father God: the gift of faith. Faith must inform and permeate all our thinking, all our desires, all our actions, personal, family, and social. Because we received the faith, we must go straight to the Truth, without hesitation, along the middle way, always defending the Church's teaching wherever we may be.

Teach them the spirit of hope, that they may themselves have many children and bring them up in a Christian manner.

Teach them the spirit of charity, that they may desire to cooperate in the great apostolates the Church has on hands at present: the apostolates of the press, cinema, radio, television and all the media that go to make up the apostolate of forming public opinion.

Yes, teach them love of God, so that they may defend the interests of the weak; for they will have many opportunities to act as good Samaritans, healing the wounds of other men left half dead by the roadside.

Teach them human love, so that they may choose the right person to help them climb the steep hill to sanctity along the road of marriage.

Teach them fraternity, so that they may strive for unity among Christians and avoid all the petty and narrow-minded dissensions so common among the mediocre. We must do everything in our power to bring about the unity of the world. This is an important aspect of the Church's temporal mission, for Christ died 'so as to bring together into one all God's children, scattered far and wide' (John 11, 52).

Teach them prayer and mortification, without which all their efforts for men and for the world – which should be so real and genuine – will be mere lies.

Teach them humility, so that they may be enterprising and magnanimous and yet give all the glory to God.

Teach them an upright piety, so that they may find in God the source of all their aspirations and a constant impulse to seek the welfare of others.

Form their intelligence, so that they will feel that it is their concern to give direction to the development and progress of humanity.

Form their heart, so that they will be masters of the earth and not weaklings, slaves of money, slaves of power, slaves of their appetites or of the flesh.

Form their will, so that they will think and decide before making a promise, and so that they will then keep it.

Teach them austerity, so that they will learn to live by their work, having all the necessities but without gratifying mere whims.

Teach them faithfulness, so that they will not be frightened when they see others desert, nor affected by the crookedness of people who call themselves friends.

Teach them sincerity, so that their yes will be yes, and their no, no.

Teach them self-confidence, so that they will bear gracefully the heavy burden of their everyday work.

Teach them to work hard, so as to develop their talents to the full.

Teach them what freedom is, so that they will be ambitious to organise a world which will give freedom to the Church of Christ and to every man.

Teach them the human virtues, so that the grace of God may develop in their personality and yield its hundredfold.

Teach them the truth, so that they will not walk hand in hand with error, as so many foolish Catholics do.

Teach them tolerance and understanding, so that they will be able to live side by side with all men, the so-called bad, and also the so-called good with whom it is sometimes difficult to get on well, because they may consider themselves too good to allow us to join them. When Christ called Matthew to follow him, the only ones to criticise it were the so-called good of the time, the pharisees. Your children should be able to live with friends and with enemies.

The Christian rule is quite clear: great understanding with the people who are in error, but the greatest intransigence with all their errors.

Leave God to decide who is good and who is bad. Remember the Cross of Christ was raised on Calvary by the efforts of many: the Jews, the Gentiles, the good, the bad, you, me. He who is free from sin, let him cast the first stone. We are all to blame for the sorrowful event that took place on Mount Calvary on that sad Good Friday evening. Get your children to open their eyes. We

Christians are responsible, genuinely responsible, for whatever course human events take, because the cause of future events is always to be found in the present which we are living and shaping.

We Christians are concerned with all the problems of the world, from the most important political, economic, artistic or social changes, to the most insignificant individual or family affairs.

Teach them not to stand by and take refuge in a stupid 'What can *I* do?' attitude, while a pagan or sectarian minority in the country passes laws that contravene the rights of Christ in society.

Form them in such a way that they may become the nation's leaders. In the words of Pope Pius XII, I want to tell you this: 'In order to be able to develop fruitful action [we need] a selection of men with solid Christian convictions, just and sure of judgment, of practical, well-balanced disposition, true to themselves in all circumstances; men of clear and sound philosophy, of steadfast and straightforward purposes; men capable, above all, by virtue of the authority emanating from their pure conscience and widely radiating around them, of being guides and leaders, especially at times when pressing necessities overexcite the impressionability of the people, and make them more liable to be misled and to go astray; men who, in transitional periods . . . feel it doubly their duty to inject into the veins of the people and the state, consumed by the fire of a thousand fevers, the spiritual antidote of clear views, thoughtful kindliness and justice equally favourable to all, together with a straining of wills towards national union and harmony in a spirit of genuine brotherhood.'

The fruit you bear will then be splendid; for it will be a divine fruit.

Sow seeds. Sow the seeds of your life and your doctrine.

I cannot deny that the field in which you sow – I mean your children – may have many rocks, many thorns, a wide wayside, so that part of the seed may be wasted. But the seed will also fall on good ground, made fertile by the grace of God and by the uprightness, the strength and will-power of your children themselves . . . and then the fruit will be abundant. In spite of the rocks and the thorns, the fruit will overflow.

Persevere in sowing the good seed.

That good and holy grandmother – I wonder how long it will be before she is declared a saint? – never tired of saying: 'Ashamed, my son? Shame is only for sin.' And her son has repeated this phrase to his sons. Little wonder then that the grandchildren are now shamelessly valiant in putting the Lord's precepts into practice.

VICTORY

> *'In thee I will run girded: in my God I will leap over the wall. God, his way is immaculate' (2 Kings 22, 30-31).*

You know that at the end of time Christ will be the conqueror in heaven and on earth. You know that when he defeats all his enemies – as he will defeat them – he will deliver up his kingdom to his Father God, and 'the last of those enemies to be disposed is death' (I Corinthians 15, 26).

This world in which we live, our own poor earth, will not have the organised, polished appearance which it should have, until all things are subject to Christ at the end of time. So while man is alive, our poor world will always be a valley of tears and sorrows.

But nevertheless he who does not try to improve it is neither a Christian nor a man!

Many tears can be dried. Many sorrows can be wiped away. Many joys can be won.

Anyone who yields to the temptation to let the world take its own rotten course, anyone who refuses to make an effort – an energetic effort – to see Christ reign here in our world, in all our activity, private and public, is a scoundrel without faith, without hope, without love!

We all, both parents and children, rich and poor, have a duty to work – as much as the Lord may demand of us – for Christ, for the world and for men. Neither Dives, nor Pilate, nor Judas, nor the rich young man who was called by Christ but went away sad, nor the brothers of the prodigal son – for he has many brothers nowadays – will ever save the world.

'For the Christian who is conscious of his responsibility, even for the youngest . . . there can be no lazy tranquillity, nor can there be any flight, but only a struggle, a fight against all inaction and desertion in the great spiritual contest in which the prize to be won is the building, even more the very soul, of the future society' (Pius XII).

There will be difficulties, many difficulties, but you must not run away; you must not leave the field to the enemies of the Church.

You say you are afraid of the future, but you do not seem to be very concerned about shaping it. You act as stupidly as the bad student who is always complaining that the examinations are coming near, and yet cannot make up his mind to study as he should. You tell your children they have to study. Well, I say the same to you: work for the future in the present.

Tomorrow will be as we make it today; usually there are few surprises. These come when people are idle and do nothing but vainly complain about the present situation, bewailing the times that are long passed and will never return.

Those who are neutral, indifferent, passive spectators, abstentionists, partisans of 'laissez faire, laissez passer', cowards: these people are accomplices in all the iniquities and crimes committed by the enemies of God.

And you, parents, will also be to blame for the passive attitude of your children if you neglect to bring them up to act as Christians. The young people of today, like the young people of all times, will be willing to act if they are brought up to act. Saint James's warning applies to young men, mature men and old men, all alike: 'If a man has the power to do good, it is sinful in him to leave it undone' (James 4, 17). Neither prayer, nor mortification, nor good will is enough: we must have prayer, mortification and also work.

We must do our own work and also the work of others who have got tired and left it undone. We are all, whether old or young, responsible for the state of the world. It may, and unfortunately it does, happen that the majority of people neglect their duties; they get tired and abandon the work entrusted to them by God. The deserters are in a majority.

Do not stop even to look at them; continue the task; snatch the banner from them and go on ahead, as if they were dead. But remember, their work has to be done, although there are fewer of us left to do it, although the burden on each of us is heavier.

Judas's grace passed to Matthias; others must come to fill the gap left by the deserters. Those still on their feet will have to do all God's work.

Teach your children this, so that they may not be scandalised by desertions or fall into the temptation of joining the band of lazy onlookers. There have always been deserters. There have also been traitors, even in the early days of Christianity. For instance there were those two who disclosed Saint Polycarp's whereabouts when they were tortured, of whom the Acts of the Martyrs says drily: 'And those who had betrayed him suffered their due, that is to say, the punishment of Judas himself.'

Never allow cowardice or discouragement to enter your soul. Be prepared to risk everything in this struggle to win the world for Christ; it is well worth while. This is a genuine war for genuine peace; it is a war in which those who fight cannot lose. They have the Lord's promise for that; he assures them of victory, and John reminds them of it from a rocky island, where he saw the winners arriving in a new land.

For there is indeed a new land awaiting us after our victory; a new land where we will have no more death, no tears, nor thirst, nor night, nor cries, nor work (cf Apocalypse 21, 4). But for the moment we have to carry on the war. The judgment will come later. 'Before this throne', says John in the Apocalypse, 'in my vision, the dead must come, great and little alike; and the books were opened . . . And the dead were judged by their deeds, as the books recorded them.' The sea itself, death and hell, will also give up the dead they have imprisoned, to be judged according to their deeds.

Finally comes the sentence.

The sound of the day of the Lord can already be heard; the day when the deserters will weep with pain. 'Then', the Lord tells us through the mouth of Sophonias, 'I will destroy men from off the face of the land . . . I will destroy out of this place the remnant of Baal . . . and them that turn away from following the Lord.'

On the day of the Lord all those who have worn foreign garments will be punished. Neither their gold nor their silver will save them. The Lord will be terrible against them. He will wipe out all the gods on earth. And the proud cities who said in their heart: 'I, and I alone' will be razed to the ground, and become dens of wild beasts. With the fire of his zeal the whole earth will be consumed.

But for those who trust in the Lord, Saint John tells us, he will be their God and they will be his children. Of this we are assured by the Prince of the kings of the earth, the Firstborn of the dead, the All-powerful, him who has fire in his eyes and whose voice is like the sound of many waters, who holds the keys of death and of hell, who died and returned to life, who holds the seven stars in his right hand:

'Who wins the victory? Who will do my bidding to the last? I will give him authority over the nations; to herd them like sheep with a crook of iron.

'Who wins the victory? I will feed him with the hidden manna, and give him a white stone, on which stone a new name is written.

'Who wins the victory? His name I will never blot out of the book of life, his name I will acknowledge before my Father and his angels.

'Who wins the victory? I will make him a pillar in the temple of my God. I will write on him the name of my God.

'Who wins the victory? The Star of morning shall be his.'

The Son of God says: 'I am the Lord, who search the heart and prove the reins. I have no fresh burden to lay upon you; keep hold of what is in your grasp already until I come.'

Let us make good use of our time now, before it runs out. Let us take full advantage of it today, because tomorrow we will have one day less. Let us use it properly, before it is too late.

Let us make good use of our time before the apocalyptic Angel appears, that Angel who carries a bow in his hands and puts one foot in the sea and the other on the land, because then he will cry out: 'Time will be no more.'

Meanwhile, and it is Saint Paul who tells you this, 'you must play a part worthy of Christ's Gospel . . . This must be my news of you, that you are standing fast in a common unity of spirit, with the faith of the Gospel for your common cause. Show a bold front at all points to your adversaries' (cf Philippians 1, 27-28).

Everything the Lord has promised you will be fulfilled. In fact, it will all be far better and greater than you ever dreamed.

Parents, your children and this world of yours are worth all your efforts. It is well worth while continuing to be faithful to the vocation you have received as parents. The world will be transformed when the homes of the world are transformed. After the struggle and the weariness, victory will come. And after the victory will come God's reward for his children.

[1] Cf *Man's Religious Sense* by Giovanni Battista Montini, London 1961